J.D. *to* J.D.

MY JOURNEY FROM JUVENILE DELINQUENT
TO DOCTOR OF JURISPRUDENCE

BRIAN D. CAPLAN, ESQ.

BRAIG PUBLISHING INTERNATIONAL

Print: 978-0-578-62697-0
Ebook: 978-0-578-62699-4

Published by Braig Publishing International

Book and cover design by Creative Management Partners
Manufactured in the United States of America

ACKNOWLEDGMENTS

I would like to thank my wife Emilie for many years of compassion, understanding, support, and adventures.

Thanks to my editors over time, including the late Hillel Black, who encouraged me to write this book, followed by David Wilk and Jeremy Townsend, whose guidance has been invaluable.

I would like to thank my sister Michelle, who has a heart of gold, and who can laugh with me, reminiscing about the childhood we endured.

Thanks to my son Reid, who has helped me grow as a person and who has led by example, demonstrating courage, resilience and perseverance, as well as a commitment to helping persons with disabilities.

Lastly, I would like to thank the friends in my life who have listened to my storytelling, shared fun times, and have made my life richer:

Mark Arisohn and Diane Alexander

Marc Gordon and Carolyn Porter

Rob and Deirdre Gale

Paul LiCalsi and Wendy Jeffrey

Gary and Lorrie Puckett

John and Alejandra Bradley

Joe Serling and Merril Wasserman

Jay, Jagi, and Pami Panda

Craig and Heather Langer

Nick Ferrara

and Kenville John (KJ)

CONTENTS

TURNING TO A STRAIGHT AND NARROW PATH

LIFE AS AN ENTERTAINMENT LAWYER

PREFACE

We never know how important it is to have parents as guiding lights. I count myself among some of the luckiest people alive today. I didn't win the lottery or a Nobel Prize. But my life, once spiraling out of control and heading for the abyss, was resurrected and redirected. With no parental supervision to speak of, I was once the wild child with no moral fiber. I could have as easily become a habitual criminal as any other vocation. But I received a second chance, went on a straight and narrow path, through law school, then a legal career in the entertainment industry. Turns out that many of my childhood experiences and encounters gave me invaluable training on how to assess and interact with others. Thirty-five years later, clients I never would have dreamed of counseling come to me for advice. I have been honored to represent the estates of George Gershwin and James Brown, the Allman Brothers Band, and Tempo Music, Duke Ellington's publishing company, to name a few. Anything is possible if you put your mind to it and have a bit of luck. The moral of the story: don't ever give up or feel sorry for yourself. Keep on truckin'.

Brian Caplan, January 2020

VIGNETTES
FROM
MY YOUTH

1.

My First Arrest at Age Twelve

It was a muggy and overcast day in Manhattan, September 1972. Manuel, my Portuguese neighbor who was the son of the "super" in my building, and I had turned twelve. By twelve, we had seen crimes, even a murder victim. We had seen all walks of life in the Village: men, women, and anything in between. Vietnam War protestors, flower children, hippies, rich and poor people of all colors and religions had passed our way. Being twelve on the streets of Greenwich Village wasn't like being twelve on the prairie farms of Nebraska. It wasn't like being twelve in the slums of Delhi. It wasn't like being twelve on the streets of Lucerne, Switzerland, where you could eat right off the sidewalk. At twelve in Greenwich Village, we "ruled"—or so we thought.

Actually, Manuel and I lived on 16th Street and Sixth Avenue (Avenue of the Americas), which technically was the Chelsea section of Manhattan. But Greenwich Village sounded cooler and we were cool. Despite our occasional street thug mentality, Manuel and I were truly wet behind the ears. My personal rap sheet was a short dime novel. I had been nabbed for the first time "borrowing" Hot Wheels cars from the local Woolworth store on 67th and Amsterdam when I was nine. I never quite figured out how I got caught with four nifty three-inch cars that could do the loop-the-loop on the Hot Wheels track, while the six-year-old brother of my partner in crime, Kevin from the projects, made it out unscathed with a three-foot-long new Tonka truck. Well, justice is blind. My clean-cut dad received the call from the Woolworth manager and was asked to pick me up and bring any Hot Wheels cars lying around our apartment that he hadn't purchased for me. Dad, the goddamn "do-gooder," brought two shoeboxes filled with cars back to Woolworth. I was convicted on the spot. No Miranda warnings or nothing.

By age twelve, I was hard core. My personal accomplishments included pocketing penny candy from Bertha's "Jip Joint" on Sixth Avenue between 10th and 11th, adjusting the bottle playing spin the bottle in Washington Square Park (when nobody was looking) in order to kiss the prettiest girl, and stealing the skeleton from science class, dropping it from my second story window at three a.m. on Halloween in 1971, (resulting in a hobo fainting on the sidewalk). At twelve, Manuel and I were both tough and we would do what was necessary to prove it. We didn't have chips on our shoulders. We had bricks. We knew everything. Nobody was smarter or more cunning. And we had our blades. The knives of choice in the early 1970s in lower Manhattan were penknives, lock blades, switchblades, or stilettos. Penknives were for wimps, lock blades took too much time to open in a pinch, switchblades were cool, and stilettos were cooler.

In September of '72 I was already a man; I had lost my virginity (or gained my pride) about a month earlier. My sister's babysitter was eighteen and healthy. She had her boyfriend's initials carved into her arm. I guess she had short-term memory loss. She was attractive in a Mata Hari type of way. Long hair, dark complexion . . . and hey, I was twelve, so anybody looked good. The circumstances underlying my first carnal knowledge are somewhat of a blur. All I remember is that the room was dark, it didn't take long, and I was happy when it was over. What was in it for her, I'll never know.

On this particularly fine day, Manuel and I, stickball and stickball bat in hand, decided to play stickball on "our court" at a vacant parking lot on the northeast corner of 15th Street and Sixth Avenue. Like dogs marking their territory, we had spray-painted a box on a wall for the batter's box and a line on the ground some sixty feet away, as the pitcher's rubber. With our blades in tow, we took the short walk to our court, the outline of the batter's box still visible on the concrete wall. Two ten- or eleven-year-old "faggots," what we called anybody we didn't like (with no homosexual connotation) were on our court. Our territorial integrity had been violated. Manuel and I didn't miss a beat. We coolly walked up to the chumps, pulled out our switchblades, opened them in unison and jointly said, in two-part harmony mind you, "If you're here when we get back, you're dead." We walked a block to our local pizza joint, downed a couple of slices and were ready for action. Sure enough, when we got back to our court, those trouble-making wimps were gone.

Not cognizant of our social transgressions, we quickly were in heated competition. Manuel, the better pitcher between us, clenched the pink Spalding ball tightly. He wanted to blow me away with his prowess. Fastball high and tight followed by a curveball away, then a sinker. If I guessed right, I nailed it, if not I whiffed. On my third out we switched places. As I was practicing my Nolan Ryan fastball, I heard a couple of sirens in the distance but didn't think twice about them. Next thing I knew, two cruisers were upon us. I turned around. The cop car on the left stopped right in front of me, and with its hard rubber bumper, pushed me slowly to the wall, about sixty feet away. In a flash, the cops were out of their cars, guns drawn. A combination of shock and awe ensued. Directions given, Manuel and I were facing the wall, legs spread, arms apart, being frisked. Damn, they got my knife. His too. Shit! My arms were pulled behind my back and I heard the clicks of the handcuffs as they closed tightly around my wrists. I saw Manuel being cuffed as well.

Out of habit, the officer pushed my head down as he shoved me into the back seat of the cruiser. Of course, with my size he didn't need to adjust for my head. Manuel was next. It wasn't until I was in the back of the police car, hands tightly cuffed, staring at the metal grating separating driver from back seat passengers, that reality hit me. I was scared shitless. As a middle-class youth I didn't know how this could be happening to me. I wanted to say I was like "Big Julie" from Chicago in *Guys and Dolls* and that I had a clean record reflected by my eighteen arrests and not one conviction, but I was too scared to joke.

Manuel did not say a word. His dark Portuguese complexion had lost its color. He was ashen, terrified more about what his strict father would do to him when he found out, than what the cops could possibly do. A belt lashing was looming in his future.

We were thrown into the cruiser of the "I Spy" team. One white and one black officer of the law. Where the hell were they taking us anyway?

"Your asses are ours."

"Do you already have a J. D. card, or will this be your first?"

"You guys messed up."

"This will follow you the rest of your lives."

"A few days in the lock-up will be good for you."

"Yeah, it will teach them a lesson."

The knot in the pit of my stomach was getting tighter. My head started to hurt.

We were taking the long way to the 10th Precinct on 20th between Seventh and Eighth avenues. The streets were a blur.

"Do you know the meaning of a J. D. card? It follows you for life."

"Your parents will love you for this one."

Manuel gulped. I heard his stomach gurgle and turn over like the sound one hears when the plunger frees up the clogged toilet and the water finally drains down. The same sound you can hear about ten minutes after winning the bet that you can eat a raw hot chili pepper.

I always thought that there was supposed to be a good cop and a bad cop. But these guys were apparently both bad and I wasn't too happy about it.

"Boy that piss smell in the lock-up can really get to you."

"Who's in there today? Jimmy?"

"Yeah, he really likes young boys, doesn't he?"

It seemed as if it took forever to get to the Precinct. I choked back the taste of pizza as it made a surprise appearance. Who else had been in this seat before? I wondered. It wasn't a pretty sight.

The police cars were all parked head first perpendicular to the police station as we pulled up. Truly an ominous sight. I gagged. The metal divider shimmered and confirmed my confinement was not fleeting. Robert Culp opened my door. Bill Cosby opened Manuel's door. My heart was racing. I felt chilled. The color still gone from Manuel's face.

As the officers exited the vehicle, I heard Cosby say, "Do you think we should give these losers another chance?"

Culp responded, "Why would we want to do that? I know their kind. We'll just have to lock them up some other day."

"You really think so?"

Culp: "Yeah."

As they had helped push us into our seats before, now they pulled us out, cuffs first, Manuel from the right of the vehicle, me from the left.

"Before today, we never saw your sorry asses before. You don't think we will ever see them again, do you?"

Quick to reply, I said: "No sir."

Manuel was still incapable of connecting his brain to his vocal chords.

"Okay, then consider yourself lucky. You've been given one break. You will not get another."

Manuel and I stood silent. Gazing like deer shocked by oncoming headlights with no idea which way to turn. Lost in the moment. Too much was happening too fast. Could it be true that we were out of harm's way?

As our handcuffs were being opened, an air of relief overcame us. Manuel began to let go of the thoughts of his father's ire. I could breathe again without the gripping feeling in the pit of my gut.

"Now get out of here."

The cuffs were off. We were free. Manuel and I took a few steps away from the cruiser heading toward Seventh Avenue. Then I hesitated for a second, turned to two of New York's finest and diminutively asked, "Do you think I could have my knife back?"

Manuel looked on incredulously and without hesitation whacked me upside my head making a loud noise as if he had hit something hollow. Next thing I knew Manuel and I were running away. We didn't look back, but we knew we weren't being chased either. Now we could laugh. And we did, all the way home.

2.
The Class Clown

Our personalities are often shaped by the environments in which we are raised. When you don't receive enough love and nurturing as a child you can compensate for it in many different ways. You can be bitter, insecure, self-destructive or a thrill seeker, or you can seek attention, approval, and affection from those around you. I was destined to take the latter approach. As soon as I was old enough to be recognized as a class clown, I became one. I was the wisecracker in the back of the classroom, always on hand to turn a phrase or make an editorial comment. I thought I was skilled at making others laugh and was proud of my perceived skill.

Using humor as a tool to connect with others, I routinely challenged the authority of my teachers during the process. As if auditioning for a standup comedy routine, I would entertain my peers in fifth, sixth, and seventh grade, pushing the limits with my elders. I was the comedic troublemaker looking for trouble. "Ns" and "Us" were scattered around my semiannual report cards, always in red, signifying that I "needed improvement" or that my behavior was simply "unsatisfactory" in class. Unlike most of my peers, I thought my red grades in behavior were something to be proud of. I was sure that Lou Costello, Stan Laurel, and Moe from the Three Stooges had all gotten "Ns" and "Us" on their report cards, and they hadn't turned out half bad.

From elementary school through high school, I pushed the pedal to the metal and made it my quest to make others laugh. In order to be successful, you needed to rapidly assess your audience, determine how to tickle their funny bones, and then deliver the punch lines. Being the class clown was not for the faint of heart. You needed to have confidence in your own abilities and know that not every attempt at humor would hit pay dirt. Even Johnny Carson would throw in a clunker every once in a while, and it didn't hurt his routines.

Little did I know at the time, but the training I endured as a class clown taught me important skill sets to be an attorney and to interact with others. Studies have shown that class clowns often grow up to be adults who have leadership skills; have a cheerful disposition; have high self-esteem and a good sense of humor; and who are independent. These adult class clowns are also positive thinkers, task-oriented and better than most at problem-solving.

I am sure there was at least one negative character trait for the class clown in adulthood, but I have forgotten it now.

3.
New York City Rank-Out Contests, Training for the Future

Growing up in the New York City public school system had its share of challenges. Learning how to hold your own in "rank-out" contests was one of them. The rapid-fire trading of insults and barbs with your peers was an acquired skill. Before rap battles such as those featured in the film *8 Mile* were a thing, the schoolyard and cafeteria were battlegrounds in the 1970s for boys and girls ages nine to thirteen in the Big Apple. Intellectual prowess did not come into play. Verbal agility, a quick wit, and thick skin were the touchstone characteristics required to prepare you for combat. Nothing was off limits. Mothers, body parts, sports ability or the lack thereof, looks, finances—you name it and it could be the springboard for a dig. Rank-out contests were a multiracial, multiethnic pastime.

Like the momentum of a speeding train, exchanges ensued. There was no height advantage. The little guys could hang with the basketball stars. Words were the equalizers. Nobody had a home court advantage, but all participants had a built-in audience: our classmates.

Yo mama so fat, she has her own zip code.

Yo mama so ugly, she made an onion cry.

Yo mama so ugly she don't need a mask on Halloween.

Did you get the license plate number of the car that ran over your face?

Your dick is so small, when you pee you water your balls.

Yo mama wears combat boots.

Yo mama's like a door knob, everybody gets their turn.

The cockroaches are so big in your house, the rats have to carry switchblades.

How many times have your parents moved without telling you their new address?

Yo mama's so low she can play handball on the curb.

You so short my dog mistook you for a fire hydrant.

You so ugly, it hurts to look at you.

If we dropped yo mama and a pig from the top of the Empire State Building, which one would land first? Who cares!

Yo mama so ugly, when you were born they put blinders on you to save your sight.

Do you know why fucking dogs is illegal? Because we don't need any more of your family members crawling around the neighborhood.

You're so low you can play Tarzan from your shoelaces.

When God was giving out brains, you thought he said trains and missed yours.

The lights are on, but nobody's home.

If we took your IQ card and multiplied it by three it would still be a negative number.

When God was giving out looks, you thought he said books and didn't want any.

If you were any uglier, you would be breaking the law.

When you were born the doctor smacked your face instead of your ass because he couldn't tell the difference.

To the victor goes the spoils. Rank-out contests would continue until the audience got weary or the wordsmiths ran out of retorts. Generally, both sides would claim victory, walk their separate ways and await the next encounter.

During my tenure at P.S. 41 and I.S. 70 in Greenwich Village and the Chelsea section of Manhattan from 1970 to 1972, I received straight As in rank-out contests. Although they did not factor into my grade point average, they did prepare me for the future.

4.

Taking on the Bully,
Gaining Some Respect

In 1970, when I was ten years old, my mother gained custody of my sister and me following her divorce from my father and two lengthy stays in psychiatric hospitals, the first when I was five, the second when I was eight. My thirty-year-old mother possessed limited disciplinary skills, and I quickly took advantage of my surroundings, generally coming and going as I pleased. Greenwich Village in 1970 was a mecca for divorcees, anti-war protestors, flower children, artists, and transients. Kids grew up really fast there, many playing spin the bottle and trying marijuana by age eleven or twelve. I was no exception, often returning home in the wee hours to find my mother asleep, with a test pattern and high-frequency humming noise blaring from the television after the networks went off air.

I attended P.S. 41 on 11th Street between Sixth and Seventh avenues. Most of my classmates came from one-parent households. We had a very progressive teacher named Mr. Smith, who entertained us with his unusual Jamaican dialect.

"Please cease and desist from masticating with your mandibles in my domicile," meant no gum chewing in the classroom.

Mr. Smith was a disciplinarian and ran a tight ship. You could only bring snacks into class if you brought enough for everyone. Note passing, giggling, and daydreaming were strictly forbidden.

P.S. 41, a public school for first to fifth graders, was very civilized. On the other hand, I.S. 70, a breeding ground for sixth through ninth graders, was a different story. Located not far away, I.S. 70 was in a decrepit, overcast building moldering away and home to many tough characters. Cut-off shirts showing muscles, do-rags worn by some (before they were in vogue years later) and no dress code. Many brawls took place. As in *Lord of the Flies*, the weak were set upon by the strong and aggressive. And the meek will inherit the Earth? I think not. There were no metal detectors to deter "carrying" in those days. Beatdowns were a common occurrence. The weak were required to give over their lunch money to the holdup artists who were white, black, or Puerto Rican—equal opportunity offenders.

"Show me the whites of your pocket."

"Take off your sneakers and show me you ain't got no money hidden in your shoes. 'Cause if you do, it's mine."

There were cliques of bad dudes you wanted nothing to do with. Until you were tested in a public forum and came out on top, you were a target and potential victim.

You didn't always have the opportunity to prove yourself and if you tried with the wrong guy or group you were in trouble. Sometimes luck is more important than wisdom. On occasion fights were avoidable. Other times they were not. My initiation came early on.

It was the first week of sixth grade in my new school. I was just getting familiar with my surroundings. The bell rang, signaling the change of classes. We had approximately five minutes to move from one classroom to another. When the bell rang again the hallway monitors swept the dillydalliers to their assigned destination. Kids talked, congregated, and walked at various paces through the hallways, some in groups, some alone. The bell rang and I was moving from English to math, room 201 to 306. Two of my classmates walked with me.

As I approached a set of swinging doors going one way, the door on the left swung open and a kid with a muscle shirt, talking to three guys, walked through. As he saw me he intentionally crossed the imaginary median in the hallway, turned his body to an angle, and rammed his left shoulder into my chest while at the same time saying:

"Watch the fuck where you're going."

I instinctively put my hands up to repel him off me. The show then began.

"Who the fuck do you think you are?"

"Do you think you own this hallway?"

"Do you think you're better than me?"

My classmates backed away and watched the commotion. My combatant didn't stop.

Before I could get a word in edgewise, two teachers were pulling us away from each other.

"Don't think this is over."

"We are going to settle this after class."

"I will be waiting."

"Your ass is mine."

Before I could even figure out what was happening I had become the subject of an after-school fight. Turns out that these non-pay-per-view events generally took place in the schoolyard. And somehow even without use of the school's PA system, everybody learned about these call-out fights.

My once and future assailant was Eric Dworfman, a fairly scrawny loudmouth troublemaker. He was a seventh grader who only picked on people his own size or smaller. He used his motormouth and tough talk to intimidate people. Eric usually did this bullying in an entourage. He had to perform in the hallway for his boys or else he wouldn't belong anymore.

In the lunchroom an hour later people started pointing at me even before Eric arrived on the scene. A tall kid named Johnny C., who had attention deficit disorder before they knew there was such a thing, walked by me and said, "I heard your ass is grass after class."

To eleven- and twelve-year-old boys and girls, a scheduled fight after class is more exciting than Ali versus Frazier. You're there in the moment screaming for blood. It doesn't matter who wins, just hope it's a long fight and that somebody gets a beating.

The afternoon classes seemed to take an eternity. My mind was floating, and I didn't feel too good. There was no way out. Me and the "mouth" had to get it on. None of my classmates talked to me, as if they didn't want to interfere with my focus, just Johnny C., repeating: "Your ass is grass after class." It wasn't time for last rites yet.

The bell signaling the end of the day's final period finally rang. *High Noon* at three p.m., with Gary Cooper walking down Main Street in the deserted town and "Do Not Forsake Me Oh My Darlin'" playing in the background. Or was it Burt Lancaster in *Shootout at the O.K. Corral?* I slowly worked my way out of the building not knowing what fate had in store for me, but it was my time of reckoning.

Eric was already in the schoolyard waiting for me. He had his team with him and many onlookers clamoring for a good brawl. During the opening days of the Civil War in 1861 many well-to-do couples took carriage rides to Manassas Junction, a stone's throw away from Washington, DC, to witness the first real military engagement between the North and the South, picnics in tow. As voyeurs they expected a quick and decisive Union victory to end the war. Instead they saw their boys get thoroughly trounced in the "Great Skedaddle."

No history was being made this day. Just a brawl between me and Eric Dworfman. As I approached Eric, everybody in the general area gathered and formed a circle of humanity around us, such that we were encapsulated with no place to go. People began screaming things, but I couldn't hear anything clearly. The young crowd pined for blood. My mind was in a frenzy, my stomach was in a knot. I walked closer and Eric yelled some profanity at me. He otherwise did not have much of a vocabulary to speak of. He lunged and struck my arm. I moved back and he tried again. I returned the fire and grazed his head with my right fist. Now who was the gladiator and who was the lion? The coliseum was erupting.

"Get him."

"Kick his ass."

"Knock him upside his head."

"Beat the shit out of him."

Eric threw a roundhouse punch that missed my chest but nailed my right shoulder.

I veered away in a defensive posture.

Didn't seem like anyone was rooting for either of us. They just wanted action.

Eric came at me again, swinging wildly. This time I maneuvered on an angle and was able to grab him in a bear hug, locking my arms around his body and arms, tripping in the process, we both fell to the cement ground. I didn't let go, and we rolled over a few times. When we came to a rest, I was on top and was able to manipulate my knees to hold down Eric's arms. I got in two or three punches to Eric's face, giving him a bloody nose just before a teacher pulled me off and another adult restrained Eric as we stood facing each other.

The kids got their money's worth. Now the school authorities were dealing with the aftermath. I was in a daze and Eric was clearly humiliated. His bark was louder than his bite. I was escorted back into the school, given a lecture that I do not remember, and then permitted to go home. Although I looked over my shoulder at least a few times on the four-block walk home, fearing potential retribution, I had a determined and purposeful gait with a feeling of accomplishment. I had been tested and had prevailed.

During my next two years at I.S. 70, I really didn't get tested again. People who didn't even witness the engagement had heard about it. Eric invited me to be one of his boys, which I tactfully declined. The weak kids respected me, and the tough kids let me be.

On one occasion I was walking down a hallway alone and a big kid who I was unfamiliar with was opening and closing his lock blade with a flip of the wrist. When he came upon me, he kept his blade open and demanded money. From the extreme end of the hallway a deep voiced yelled out: "Leave him alone, he's cool."

And as quickly as that, the blade was closed, and my assailant walked on.

When first interacting with individuals who are physically intimidating or psychologically domineering, I learned that one must set the appropriate tone from the beginning. If you are fearful or allow yourself to get bullied, you cannot change the dynamic of the relationship down the road. If you present yourself as strong and unafraid, you are a lot less likely to be trampled upon or taken advantage of.

Later in life, when I became an attorney, this lesson served me well.

5.
Do You Wanna Bet?

Gambling is the purest and most ideal form of escapism that exists. If you are looking to get away from your worries without taking a trip, neither alcohol nor drugs will do the trick. Drunk or stoned, your anxieties will leak through and can even be exacerbated in your vegetative state. Gambling, on the other hand, immerses you in the thrill or excitement of the moment to the exclusion of your daily frets, significant or trivial. Whether in a poker game or watching a sporting event where you have action, you don't think of anything else.

While I did not have a deck of cards in the womb with me for nine months, I was a numbers guy and a risk taker from a very young age. Starting with the game war at five and moving on to gin rummy and spit by seven, followed by poker, blackjack, bridge, and hearts from eight through ten, I was a quick study and ready to play. My earliest recollection of a wager was when I was eight, in third grade, at a friend's house after school, playing poker for baseball cards. Each game took on a series of debates as bets had to be made and matched by comparable cards. A Willie Mays for a Mickey Mantle. Stan Musial for a Yogi Berra. Whitey Ford for Bob Gibson. Anybody for Ed Kranepool. We also flipped for cards. If the second flipper matched the first flipper's heads or tails, he would win the card thrown. If he flipped tails after heads was flipped, he would lose. Back then the condition of the card was of no importance.

By age eleven, I was playing poker and blackjack with select friends for silver coins, Indian head pennies, comic books, baseball cards, and "rocks," also known as collectible minerals. If you had listened in on some of those games, you would have thought we were demented.

"I will see your quartz crystal and raise you a chunk of galena."

"I will see your galena and raise you a small geode and piece of pyrite."

I graduated to playing cards for cash at age twelve and backgammon by fourteen. At fifteen, I was allowed to join a regular bi-weekly poker game run by some of the more popular tenth graders at Sheepshead Bay High School in Brooklyn. After winning on multiple occasions, I was not asked back.

It was at fifteen that I took my first foray into sports betting. One of my classmates, E. F., had a bookie and was serving as his runner and local agent. E. F. was passing on action from our high school classmates to his bookie on Saturday and Sundays for college and pro-football games. He was also distributing and collecting football sheets and taking a commission. A football sheet listed many college and pro-football games with the point spreads for each. You could pick a minimum of three games, up to a maximum of eight games, but had to win all your selections to have a winning ticket. A tie was as good as a loss when picking. A one-dollar bet returned five if you hit three for three. Ten dollars was the return for four for four, and so on. The odds were stacked in the bookie's favor. A few months into the school year I was at the right place at the right time and was hired to hand out the sheets for a twenty-percent commission. It was not long before I was selling five hundred to six hundred dollars a week in tickets, earning a hundred plus in commissions and using that as my bankroll for other betting ventures. I graduated to betting directly on sporting events with the bookie shortly thereafter.

Gambling may not be the root of all evil, but it surely isn't a virtue. Done in moderation it won't kill you. It will only make your pockets a little lighter.

In life there are risk takers and those that are conservative. I was not the conservative type.

6.

Mastering the
Five Finger Discount

Five finger discounts or petty larceny was a part-time pastime. The adrenaline rush was not in the value of the item taken, but in the risk associated with the act. In my youth, I never stole anything of value: collectible postage stamps from Macy's, pink Spalding balls from Paragon, candy from the local store on Sixth Avenue between 10th and 11th, and rocks and shells from the nature store. The trick to the offense was to hide the targeted object on my body, act completely natural, and buy one item on the way out of the store.

While I may have been a bit more brazen in high school and college, the opportunities to exercise my talent were few and far between. Other than one wayward night in college where, upon a dare, a companion and I absconded with an ugly couch and an uglier love seat from a dormitory floor, all of my transgressions were directed at stores, not individuals. I never thought I was doing anything wrong. I simply wanted to see if I could get away with it. I was never officially caught, except that one time when I was eight with pockets full of Hot Wheels cars.

Thrill seeking comes in all shapes and sizes. When the billionaire cheats on his tax return simply ask yourself, why?

7.
Parenting in the Balance:
No Licensing Test Required

Upon my birth I was thrust upon my parents and they were thrust upon me. Unfortunately, you don't get to choose your parents as you might choose a car off an assembly line. Give me the Mercedes-Benz 450 SL with the convertible top, leather tan interior, bucket seats. It doesn't work that way. You are born and there they are. They don't take any qualifying exam, no certification is required, and they are exempt from any state or federal licensing requirements. They don't need to obtain a minimal educational level or have past employment experience to fill the position. Parents do not even have to pass a rudimentary physical or mental exam. In fact, there isn't even a minimum age requirement; you can be fourteen and legally give birth. Life experiences and your own upbringing may prepare you for parenthood. Many just try to play the roles, oblivious to reality. But life is not a dress rehearsal, and one's ability to nurture and teach as a parent will only be tested by time. There is no magic formula for parenting, nor is there a prescription for success. Unlike the Mercedes-Benz, you can't trade in a parent for a new model. Parents are yours for life, until death.

My parents would have failed a standardized parenting exam given by New York State had one existed. Each was raised by a stoic and domineering mother, where warmth came only from a wool blanket. Neither one rarely if ever received positive reinforcement or TLC in their youths. Their fathers, one a well-respected doctor and the other an innovative toy manufacturer who cofounded Creative Playthings (a successful toy company in the 1940s through the 1960s), escaped from their outspoken, controlling mates, and sought refuge in their professions (and possibly other women).

When you have a childhood devoid of real affection, it is impossible to predict the outcome. One can be bitter against the world. One can be self-absorbed. One can be insecure or, one can learn to adapt. Having been likely born with a predisposition for mental illness, my mother's childhood surroundings did not bode well for her. By her early teens she was manifesting signs of significant depression, which drove a wider schism between her and her parents. My father's mother, a perfectionist, never met a person, subject or inanimate object she couldn't criticize. Accordingly, nothing my father could do would generate the approbation he needed from her in his youthful environment.

As their teens moved into early adulthood, Mom and Dad both excelled intellectually and scholastically, but nothing had trained them for parenthood. Swarthmore and Haverford College, elite schools outside Philadelphia, would facilitate their professional accomplishments. However, neither took "intro to parenting." Having married while in college to rebel and gain independence from their parents, Mom and Dad were ready to escape to a new world, a world where their mothers would not dominate, and their fathers would not leave them unprotected. What better way to get away than to start a family? A baby changes everything . . . and can make you an adult before your time. Or so they thought. When the fateful day came and I was born in 1960, they were twenty and twenty-one years of age, and ill-equipped for the challenge. Although both were well-tempered, each was young and egocentric, and neither had the ability to nurture. They ultimately failed their parenting exam, but were not left back, nor did they lose any rights or privileges.

As a result of my relationship with my parents, I adapted to life by becoming independent, self-reliant, and a consummate entertainer of people, constantly seeking out social interaction.

8.
Drug Dealing 101—
Learning Supply-and-Demand
Economics at Age Fifteen

Robert Blake portraying Baretta said, "Don't do the crime unless you can do the time."

As an invincible yute (as they say in Brooklyn), there was no way I was going to get caught for buying and selling drugs. Couldn't happen. I was smart. The supplier only wanted your cash, so how could buying be a problem? The users only wanted your product, so how could selling be a problem?

Dealing was simply a matter of supply-and-demand economics, with the need to have access to the supply. While you needed to risk breaking the law selling, the consumer believed he was only committing a transgression by personal consumption of a controlled or illegal substance.

I had smoked pot for the first time when I was eleven, sitting in Washington Square Park in Greenwich Village during an anti-Vietnam War protest. An older man handed me the lit marijuana cigarette when I was sitting cross-legged in a big circle of people listening to a man with a megaphone in the distance bash President Nixon and the ill-fated war effort. It seemed natural, even if I didn't fully comprehend what was transpiring in Southeast Asia. It was like a peace pipe.

Given the open defiance of the law in daylight in a public setting with no repercussions, it appeared to be no different from trying a cigarette for the first time. My first few tokes put me in a haze and I felt like an explorer hiking through an untraveled forest.

Following my discovery of pot for transcendental purposes,

I observed the business end of the agricultural product. Nickel and dime bags passed hands repeatedly throughout the park, with impunity to the dealers even when the police were only a stone's throw away. While there had not yet been any discussions about decriminalizing marijuana, the men in blue seemed to turn a blind eye toward its sale. It looked like easy money. At age eleven, having no ability to make any real money for a capital investment into a new business venture, my foray to become an entrepreneur would have to wait a bit.

Although the frequency with which I smoked pot increased from age eleven to fourteen, thoughts of buying quantities of marijuana for resale did not cross my mind until later.

As a result of my marketing, distributing, and collecting football sheets for the local bookie, I knew many of my high-school peers. It was not a difficult transition from providing one service to them then moving to another.

Having moved to Brooklyn during the summer of 1973 before the commencement of eighth grade, I made many contacts during my first two years there. Picking up half ounces and ounces of pot for me and my friends was a common occurrence. As my patronization of one particular dealer became more frequent and disruptive to his family home with his parents, he offered that I take larger quantities of pot on consignment. At the time, pounds of average marijuana (generally of Columbian origin) were selling for three hundred fifty to four hundred dollars each. Ounces on the other hand were selling for forty dollars. Since I was not "fronting" any money for the pot, my local reliable dealer offered me a pound on consignment for four hundred and sixty dollars. This meant if I sold sixteen ounces at forty dollars each I would generate six hundred and forty dollars for him and one hundred and eighty dollars profit for my pocket. A no-brainer. I was in business and remained so for the next six years through my graduation from college.

Over the years my drug store supplied pot, hashish, black beauties (speed), Quaaludes and, on rare occasions, cocaine. Drug dealing does not take place without risks and consequences. In high school, a disgruntled purchaser who believed the product he had acquired did not live up to its billing ambushed me with two others in a drunken stupor. His accomplices pinned my arms down while he repeatedly struck me about the face, stomach, and chest, giving me a broken nose and black eye. As a violator of the law, I was not in a position to report my beating to the authorities.

As time went on I learned to vet the people to whom I sold contraband. At Brandeis University, a few years later, as an employee of its financial aid office, I handed out the paychecks to all the student employees, many of whom were my customers. In this institution of higher learning, many of my peers self-medicated to take off the edge.

The income I earned as a dealer supported my gambling habits and taking women out to fancy meals. Upon my acceptance to law school I gave up the lucrative business to pursue a more worthy vocation.

9.
A Visit to the Loan Shark

It was in my senior year at Sheepshead Bay High School that I had fallen into the habit of betting on college and pro-football games every Saturday and Sunday, studying each week's results, injury reports, and new point spreads as if it were a science. I was proud of my picking ability even if I had some off days, weeks, months, or years. My buddies and I only resorted to calling "the Professor," a paid picking service, when we were absolutely desperate for a win to bail us out of a jam. Of course, "the Professor" was only human, which meant he could not likely pick better than fifty percent of the wins in any event. But the odds for the Professor were marketed as better than those on Wall Street, enticing us to actually pay for a pick. The ads for the Professor's picks never finished with the disclaimer that "past results were no guarantee of future performance." The "Lock of the Week," a bet you can't lose, was available for a price. We all knew that there was no such thing, but it sounded so good.

November 1977 had not been kind to me. Army versus Navy, a loss. Texas against Oklahoma, the favorite didn't cover. USC versus Notre Dame, a fumble recovery for a touchdown for my opponent in the final minute. Florida versus Florida State. Fourth play from scrimmage and my quarterback breaks his finger on the defensive end's helmet. I can't catch a break. The losses were mounting, and I was gambling with money I didn't have, hoping for the big score to break even. Unfortunately, the big scores were only happening for the teams I bet against. My gambling think tank continued to come up empty. We had no Mensa members. While most weeks during the season I was up or down three to four hundred dollars at most, this week I was clobbered. Down nineteen hundred and eighty dollars with no white knight, golden parachute, or bankruptcy lawyer at my disposal. What to do? My options seemed bleak. The intermediary for the bookie, a high-school classmate of mine, said that I would not be afforded a payout schedule. "Don't do the crime, unless you can do the time," he said. Great, he had to steal a line from *Baretta*, too. Robert Blake, my hero at seventeen, being quoted to my detriment. I always envisioned Robert Conrad in his commercial for Eveready batteries, daring you to knock the battery off his shoulder, getting knocked out cold by Baretta.

Since I had no functional relationship with my custodial mother or my "old man and the sea" stepfather, I did what any blue-blooded American would do: I sought out the neighborhood loan shark. I was seventeen and still not shaving when I timidly approached the car service on Avenue X in Brooklyn that fronted for the loan sharks. When I asked the Spanish-speaking dispatcher where I might find Jimmy, the Dominican gentleman took me to see the Italian gentleman in a room in the back. Jimmy looked me up and down for a second and knew that I couldn't even legally buy a beer. I told Jimmy my tale of woe, a similar story he had probably heard five hundred times before.

"How much do you need kid?"

"Nineteen hundred eighty dollars, say two grand."

"The vig is five points per week."

"What's that?"

"It's how we make our money. Call it interest. One hundred dollars per week."

"That's a lot," I said (as I tried to figure out how I could possible pay it back). "What happens if I'm late with a payment?"

"You don't want to be late with a payment to us. When you're late, you pay and it's not in cash. We start with fingers and then move on from there."

I sat in the chair petrified and sweating. I looked down at my hands and admired my fingers. They looked good to me. No breaks, fairly straight.

Jimmy, sensing he was making an impression, and not one short on the threats, now had me in the palm of his hand. What he would do with me was solely his choice. So he decided to turn up the terror meter.

"In a real bad situation where this one punk was continually late, trying to avoid us, showing us no respect, we really had to rough him up a bit to teach him a lesson. You know what I mean, don't ya?"

He hesitated for effect. "Two of my associates paid him a visit in the Warbass projects, hung him out of the eleventh floor window by his feet and you know what?"

I sat silent, my knees trembling.

"He never missed a payment again. Funny how those things happen."

The humor was lost on me.

I thanked Jimmy for his time and said I would be back if I needed him, knowing there was no chance in hell that I would ever see Jimmy again.

My uncle bailed me out and loaned me the two grand which I paid back with interest over the next year with profits from my marijuana sales.

10.
Involuntary Commitment

I got the call about 9:45 p.m. I was on my fifth bong hit and feeling no pain. Clouds of smoke were wafting in the air. College had been good to me. Freedom and nobody to answer to. My beard was ten days old, my hair disheveled, as I sat in my room wearing an undershirt and sweats looking at my dumbbells. The words didn't quite sink in. "Your mother was committed to a state mental hospital today." The cool voice on the other end of the receiver was distant and unremarkable, disdainful as usual. An eighty-year old man in a ninety-five-year old body. Legally blind and affectionately called "Magoo" by those few who might have had any affection for him.

It was 1973 when my mother had made yet another mistake in her mate selection. A Blanche Dubois–like character, she depended on the kindness of strangers. Unfortunately, not all strangers were kind or nice. She was diagnosed manic-depressive in her mid-teens, and by age thirty-three, she didn't have the same field of male companions available to her as when she was a freshman in college. An outstanding, well-read beauty in the Natalie Wood vein, circa 1957. A great package deal at that time. But sometimes appearances can be deceiving. The passage of time had changed her.

By 1973, shock therapy and the meds had taken their toll. Thorazine, a horse tranquilizer, works wonders. My mother's confidence and self-esteem waned. Anybody who appeared to care for her was worthy of her, or so she thought. Her bedroom door had a welcome sign on it akin to a country inn. All strangers were invited. If there had been a toll collector stationed by the door, our custodial parent would have been wealthy. The revolving door had seen some interesting entrants: Arnold, the profound intellectual; Veejay, the handsome and debonair Indian computer analyst; Ciro, the "connected" Italian "family man" who was a diamond importer as a front for more nefarious activities; and Moldovan, the elderly eccentric artist, also old enough to be her father, to name a few.

During December of 1972, Mom had had a few dates with one Sam Goldstein from Brooklyn, the latest pick of the litter. On the third rendezvous, Sam did a no-show. As an outspoken twelve-year-old, I opined that he had made a wrong turn on Canal Street when looking for that perfect apple pie to bring to supper. Unable to accept rejection, my mother instructed Flo, the housekeeper and closet kleptomaniac, to call every Sam Goldstein in Brooklyn, an arduous task even for a cold caller. The phone book had a page and a half of three-columned, single-spaced S., Sam, and Samuel Goldsteins, all just waiting for that special call.

When Mom got home from a class at the Arts Student League where she was dabbling in expressionism, one of the Sam Goldsteins was on the line. Although a stranger to her, he was not for long. After a twenty-minute intro, they agreed to meet. The wrong number turned into the wrong man, but she did not think of it that way. Seven months later they were wed, to the chagrin of my grandparents. Some marry for looks, some marry for money, and some marry for true love. Others marry based upon timing and social and family pressures. Mom married to have someone to lean on, an emotional crutch. Certain people can adapt to living alone, others cannot.

It was 1973 and my sister, mother, and I moved from the laissez-faire Village to chez Sam's place in Brooklyn. Samuel Goldstein was as sensitive as a prizefighter. He had been a boxer in the roaring twenties and had had his nose broken numerous times. Jimmy Durante would have been proud of his schnozzola. From '73 to '77, Sam and I did battle. I wasn't used to anybody telling me what to do.

Sam, at five foot five, legally blind, and seventy-three years old, was not an ideal role model. His five children, all older than my mother, appreciated her intervention into Sam's life. Now they had someone to take care of their "old man."

We lived in Sam's modest home in East Flatbush, primarily a Jewish and Italian neighborhood. Brooklyn in '73 was not as enlightened as Greenwich Village. In Gerritsen Beach for example, a black family's home was firebombed as a gesture of welcome. I quickly assimilated into my new surroundings, while maintaining the openmindedness I believed I had acquired in the Village and spent as much time out of the house as possible. I networked to make new acquaintances. I started dealing pot and hashish at age fifteen and graduated to uppers and downers by seventeen.

By August of '78 I had graduated high school, was out of the house, and had moved to Waltham, Massachusetts, to attend Brandeis University.

As a Lynyrd Skynyrd "Freebird," hedonistic voices consumed me. Women (wham bam, thank you ma'am), drugs, gambling, alcohol, and any other rebellious subject matter available, I adopted. Escapism 101. I aced the class with flying colors.

It was May 1979, the end of freshman year, approaching finals. I had just exhaled the pot smoke from an exceptionally good bong toke. "Bonging" was an art form, an acquired trait that you mastered over time. The phone rang, and it was Sam.

"Your mother was committed to a state mental hospital today." Damn, not again. It had been a good seven years between visits. I was stoned and didn't want to deal. After getting the particulars and small talk out of the way, I hung up. I spent the next twenty-five minutes just staring at the bong in a transcendental meditation state . . . or was I catatonic? Marijuana was good for something.

The South Beach Psychiatric Hospital was located in "scenic"

Staten Island, a number of two-story structures with muted colors on a treeless field where all walks of life were welcome. It was Memorial Day. As I drove up to the secured grounds and waved to the security guard at the main gate, the barbed wire fence overhead gave me a feeling of confinement even before I entered. I saw a number of inmates walking around aimlessly. I parked my car in the visitors' parking lot and walked toward the main entrance with trepidation. Faces stared at me with blank expressions. I felt uncomfortable within my own skin; I didn't know whether to smile and wave back or just run away. When I got to the front desk, I asked the attending nurse which room my mother was in. Nurse Ratched's tone was desensitized and bitter as she pointed me on my way. Fourteen worn men and women stood in a disjointed line to my left, anxiously waiting, fidgeting, carrying on, complaining, and jabbering. A cigarette awaited them. One by one, they each received their dose of nicotine. With a grumble, a nod, or deafening silence, they moved to their next destination: Line two on my right was the fire line. An orderly stood patiently with a lighter as he dispensed one of the few pleasures available. With a spark, their deprivations were lost for the length of a butt. Satisfied for three or four minutes, they were passionate about their smokes. Perhaps memories of the outside filled their lungs with each breath of fresh smoke.

A short man with a pronounced twitch approached. "You're new here. What's your name?"

I hesitated. "I'm visiting someone." Ashamed to say Mom, I spit out, "My mother."

He now hesitated, uncomfortably so.

"I shouldn't be here. I don't know why I'm here. Do you know why I'm here? Can you get me out of here?" His cadence was that of an auctioneer, yet he had nothing to sell, except maybe his existence.

The short man kept talking undeterred by my failure to respond.

I asked, "Can you point me to Ward C?" My escape made easy.

"It's that way, but can't you stay and talk with me?"

"Sorry, my mother needs me."

As I scurried away, the odor of the facility hit me, an institutional smell, a disinfectant that permeates everything and everybody. My stomach began to turn. Why were these people here? Who loved them? Were their lives ever normal? Why did it smell like this?

I moved quickly toward my mother's room. It dawned on me that I was unsupervised and hadn't even shown any identification upon entering. I guess there weren't too many people trying to break in here.

When I got to room C108, the door was slightly ajar. I was scared. I didn't know what I would find on the other side. I knew I was supposed to love her no matter what. As I pushed open the door, I saw Mom sitting on the edge of her single bed dressed in a tattered flannel nightgown, her sad eyes with pronounced dark circles around them. She gazed straight ahead and did not acknowledge my presence. I just stood there. My heart sank. Mom, just thirty-eight, was a shadow of a person. Energy and spirit drained. Alive, but barely. Mom's room-mate, who appeared to be about sixty years old, was across the room sitting in a chair carrying on a conversation with herself. She spoke, then listened, nodding in approval. She spoke again this time, con-torting her face, objecting to the muted response. I bit my lip hard. A tear began to swell in my right eye. My mom looked up and said softly, "That's Sally. Don't pay any attention to her, she's harmless. Thanks for coming."

I leaned down and gently kissed my mother's forehead. "How are you doing?"

"I'm okay, I guess. But those damn lines for the cigarettes will be the end of me."

Mom had aged substantially, even in the few months since I had last seen her.

"So when you breaking out of here?" I quipped.

"I think I need to rest here a while and get my life in order."

I wanted to ask how the South Beach facility could help Mom get her life together.

Mother had expressed occasional suicidal tendencies in the depressive stage of manic depression, but I was convinced they were primarily attention-generating mechanisms. If you truly want to kill yourself, it's not that hard to succeed.

When Mom purported to want to quit life, I would tell her "tomorrow is another day, better things are in store for you. Don't give up hope."

On those occasions when she continued to engage me in a suicidal debate, or came close to convincing me that she had nothing to live for, I would strategically say, "If you want to kill yourself, then do it, but I think it's a mistake."

Deep depression and discussions of suicide landed her at South Beach. The food, cigarette lines, and inmates would drive her out.

I ushered Mom out of her dorm room setting. We both needed a walk. It was approaching three p.m. and Mom said it was almost medicine time. I followed her back to the main lounge area where the masses had started to assemble in a frenzied state. The medicinal dispensary had a half door and was available to those capable enough to get there four times a day for their "fix." As I waited with Mom, people said, "Who's the young man?"

"Got a new boyfriend now, huh."

"Oh he's cute, can I have him when you're done?"

I started to feel sick again.

As we reached the front of the meds line, the meds man gave my mother three pills and a paper cup filled with water. Knowing the routine, she swallowed the pills and drank the water down, showed the attendant her accomplishment, like a twelve-year-old proving to her mother she did what she was supposed to, and discarded the empty cup in a trash receptacle as the next man in line got his fix. Crowd control.

Sedatives to sedate, an opiate for the masses. Like medicinal religion. Where were the therapists and social workers? Could these people be helped? Mom?

As we walked toward the exit, a woman could be heard in the distance screaming.

"I want more solitary time, I want more solitary time, goddamn it, won't nobody listen to me? Answer my prayers."

I inquired, "What's solitary time?"

"Solitary time is when you are forcibly strapped down to your bed in your room." A comforting thought indeed. Mom suggested we take a walk to the facility gymnasium. As we approached the gym, a big sign was on the front door.

THIRD ANNUAL MEMORIAL DAY VOLLEYBALL GAME
COME ONE COME ALL

I opened the door to find a typical high-school gymnasium setting. A volleyball court was all set up with taped lines to mark the boundaries. A lone frail man, about fifty-five, unshaven, stood at the service line holding a volleyball. He looked around and mumbled, "Yeah, yeah, yeah," and proceeded to serve the ball. The volleyball dribbled on the ground under the net to the other side. Alone, the player remained on the service line, looked about the court for recognition, mumbled, "Yeah, yeah, yeah," and started his slow march to retrieve the ball from the other side of the court. With ball in hand, the frail man moved back to the opposing service line, appearing to try to get his wits about him, he reviewed the court again to plan the strategic placement of his next serve and mumbled, "Yeah, yeah, yeah." As he served the ball again and it dribbled under the net to the other side, I knew it was time to go. I took my mother's hand and led her away from the gymnasium. I took Mom back to her room and gave her a long warm embrace and one hundred and sixty dollars. I told her to let me know what I could do for her. She said, "Just call."

As I drove out of the South Beach facility, a sense of helplessness overcame me. I understood that no matter what my feelings were for my mother, I was powerless to effectuate any change in her day-to-day existence regardless of what I did. I had always believed that people could take control of their own lives but now it was evident that there were clearly exceptions. Even though my life had spiraled a bit out of control, and I had not yet been held accountable for my own actions, I believed I had such a capacity. My mother, on the other hand, was so fragile. Could she take control of her own life? It didn't appear likely.

My mother stayed at South Beach for fourteen months. She was released in July of 1980, and moved to the "Garden of Eden" home for adults in Brooklyn, a warehouse for those who could not help themselves. She would live in various adult homes for the next twenty years until her death at the age of sixty, an end to her suffering.

11.
Finding Religion—
Taking a Gamble on God

Karl Marx said, "Religion is the opiate of the masses." A majority of the world's population has a need for religion. However, during the history of mankind's existence, more people have been killed in the name of religious principles than any other cause. Religion in certain countries can be used to create social order. Some individuals blindly adhere to religious principles because their parents have indoctrinated them to do so. Religion and a proper upbringing can instill a sense of morality in an individual. Religion can make you reflective and retrospective. For some, religion can provide solace and inner peace; it can be an avenue of retreat when greater questions of life are not answerable with logic or reasoning.

I was not raised with any organized religion. My roots and heritage were Jewish in origin. Four grandparents, two Russian (from the areas now known as Ukraine and Belarus), one Hungarian, and one French, were all born Jewish. One grandmother converted and became a Quaker when her youthful exuberance for the principles of early communism was betrayed by Stalin's brutal conduct in the 1930s. My mother was raised as a Quaker and went to the Friends Seminary schools. My father was an agnostic Jew who didn't believe in God. Neither believed in instilling religious beliefs in their offspring. In 1968, living in Lincoln Towers in the Upper West Side of Manhattan with my father, I had six months of Hebrew school training, which was more than enough. The exercise was an attempt by my father to keep me off the street rather than the fulfillment of any wish that I did not stray from the tribe.

As irony would have it, Caplans are descendants of Cohans, the high priests of the various tribes of Israel, a group who in Orthodox circles is revered. The last thing on the radar screen I was looking for.

At age sixteen, I had been living in Brooklyn for more than three years with my thirty-six-year-old mother and Sam. I was dealing drugs on a regular basis and had become a compulsive gambler. You ran it, I would bet on it. Football, however, was my game of choice.

My best friend at the time was John L., a macho Italian kid who worked out with weights and had every hair in place. John's sister went to Catholic school, but John was spared the ordeal and permitted to attend Brooklyn public schools. As with many teenagers who have religion foisted upon them during their upbringing, John attended mandatory Sunday masses in Catholic church with his family because it was a required activity, not because he was going of his own free will. John had a tight-knit family that frequently dined together, something that I was unaccustomed to. So when I was invited to meals it was a treat and I always watched with fascination the interaction between John's strict disciplinarian father and the rest of his family.

During 1976 and 1977, John and I became really tight. *Saturday Night Fever* and the disco craze had invaded Brooklyn, and we often went clubbing wearing our flammable polyester shirts unbuttoned half-way. At seventeen, we could gain entrance to the clubs, and we happily ordered our "7 and 7s" just like Tony (John Travolta) did in the movie. When we went out on Saturday nights, we would usually take my broken-down Plymouth Gold Duster and carry a crowbar and baseball bat in the front seats just in case somebody was looking for trouble. Man, were we cool.

John and I were only two out of four people in the gambling clique. We would discuss teams, injuries, trends, and the like. It was a social event. We bonded with a common interest. During football season, we would often get together on Saturday and Sunday mornings to discuss our college and pro hunches.

In the fall of 1977, during the beginning of my senior year in high school, John's mother invited me to go to church with the family on Sunday. I asked John if that was okay and he was fine with it. The one-shot deal morphed into a trend.

Having been raised in a tumultuous environment with no real parental supervision and no ingrained morality, I attended Sunday masses with a different disposition than most. I fervently listened to the priest at the pulpit (ironically called "Father") to gain some insight into life. Morality, right from wrong, respect, conviction, principles— things I had not focused on as a self-professed "survivor." The words hit home. If Jesus being the son of God was the basis of a line of reasoning that could ultimately make me a better person, I should not reject him. So, I continued to accompany John to church on those Sundays to learn some things that I had never been taught at home.

The spirituality and warmth engendered in a room full of strangers with a common faith is a powerful device. Everyone was a brother, sister, father, mother, and didn't judge you. It is not surprising that only a few years later when my mother was committed to a state mental hospital that I obtained solace within the confines of the church. When I was accepted to law school, there was no doubt in my mind that there was a God, a God that forgave and on occasion gave you a second chance.

12.
College Campus Dealer:
A Service-Oriented Business

By age seventeen, I was a seasoned high-school pot dealer and gambler who managed to get good grades. With a manic-depressive mother and a seventy-eight-year-old, legally blind stepfather as my guardians, and college looming on the horizon, I knew I had to emigrate elsewhere. New zip codes and area codes were necessary to help bring me sanity. I didn't have a parent to help me analyze prospective universities. Instead I polled my peers. After forty-five minutes of analysis, I submitted applications to NYU, Brooklyn College, Brandeis University, Colgate, and Haverford College. I was accepted to four of the five and chose Brandeis because it was in a different state and would allow me the opportunity to attend Yankee-Red Sox games.

In August of 1978, I drove to Brandeis for the first time in a beat-up Plymouth Gold Duster to attend my first semester. I assimilated into campus life quickly, got a job at the Brandeis University financial aid office and started my own intramural flag football team. Within a few weeks, I knew a majority of the student body, and it was time to go into business.

We live by our rationalizations. As a low-level drug dealer at Brandeis University, selling to my peers, I believed I was providing a needed service. At no time did I believe I was doing anything socially or morally wrong as I was not "hurting" anyone. The fact that I was technically breaking the law was inconsequential. Using marijuana to relax was no different from drinking alcohol. Taking speed to stay awake and study was no different from drinking three cups of coffee. Quaaludes to unwind was a prescribed medication that doctors could dole out when they saw fit and had no calories compared to beer, wine, or hard liquor.

Drug dealing was also a very social activity. When my classmates wanted to score a dime bag or quarter ounce of weed, they would invariably sample the new merchandise. I wanted to make sure every customer was satisfied with their purchase. There were between five and ten dealers at Brandeis and most of the student body knew who we were. We each had our own clientele and sources, and there was never any real competition between us. We each went about our own business. Others sold cocaine, mushrooms, and hallucinogens, all of which I generally shied away from. I maintained a low profile to the extent I could and did not consummate any transactions in public, although word of mouth identified me for my additional line of business. It didn't matter that I ran track, played lacrosse, or fielded a successful intramural football team. I was a "dealer."

13.
A Quaalude Run

Quaaludes, a synthetic barbituratelike central nervous system depressant, was a very popular recreational drug in the 1970s. Also known as "gumby pills," "soapers," "714s," "lemons," and just plain "ludes," Quaaludes produced a euphoric effect within thirty to forty minutes of ingesting them, which lasted four to six hours. In college, people often "luded out" by taking a lude with wine and then just felt good.

At a retail level, ludes sold for six dollars apiece, wholesale three hundred dollars for a hundred pills. I had a few connections for Quaaludes but the demand for them generally outweighed the supply. Junior year at Brandeis I was given an opportunity to score a stash of ludes for resale on campus. My friend, MJ, and I took a road trip to the Washington, DC, area from Waltham, Massachusetts, to pick up and pay for a rather large supply of ludes. The plan was simple. We would drive seven hours there and seven hours back over one day and share the driving. In large quantities the ludes were to be offered to us at a buck apiece.

We got to Chevy Chase, Maryland, our final destination. Our supplier was waiting for us in his apartment. We sat at his round kitchen table when he came out with two large plastic bowls filled to the brim with ludes. "Start counting," he commanded. To carefully count three thousand pills took us over fifteen minutes. We paid and were back on the road.

MJ was to drive the first three-and-a-half-hour leg back and then I was to take over. We stopped at the first Dunkin' Donuts we saw and caffeinated up for the return journey. We were both tired. Only fifty minutes into our drive a vehicle with flashing red lights pulled up behind us. It was a state trooper. We hadn't been speeding, but my breath was still taken away. As we pulled to the side of the highway I said, "Just stay cool." The ludes were in the trunk in a paper grocery bag rolled up.

It was 11:30 at night.

The trooper slowly strode to the driver's side window and shined his flashlight into the car, first to the driver side, then to me, and finally scanning the back seat.

"Do you know why I pulled you over?"

MJ replied politely, "Not really."

"You changed lanes without signaling."

MJ responded, "I am terribly sorry. It won't happen again."

"Where are you guys going?"

I jumped in, "We were visiting a friend and are on our way back to college near Boston."

The trooper hesitated for a moment and said, "I am only going to give a warning this time. Just be careful driving and don't let this happen again."

As the officer walked away, we said, "Thank you," and were very happy that we had been absolutely straight and kept our wits about us.

We returned to Brandeis and sold our wares over a few weeks, making a lot of people happy and less stressed.

14.
There but for the
Grace of God Go I

It was the summer of 1979. I had just eked out my first year at Brandeis University. My Polish calculus professor, who wore the same clothing every day of the spring semester, had charitably given me a D as a grade for trying. In economics, my intellectual prowess was not much better. I received a C-. I had however mastered the concept of supply-side economics. I understood "supply and demand." If I supplied it and the student body needed it, I was ahead of the game. Freshman year I was moving about a pound of Columbian per week when the operations were cooking. Cost basis now three hundred dollars per pound as a steady purchaser. Sales at forty dollars per ounce yielded a three-hundred-forty-dollar profit for every pound. I wasn't peddling heroin outside a junior high school. I was selling pot to middle- and upper-class college kids. Didn't seem like I was doing anything wrong, and I wasn't. Drug experimentation occurred for many new college kids: uppers, downers, sidewinders, relaxants, excitants, and hallucinogens. The pill-of-the-week club replaced the book-of-the-month club. "Born to be Wild" was my theme song. I ran track, worked for the financial aid office, dealt, and everybody knew me, although my picture wasn't posted on the post office walls. Sex, drugs, and rock 'n' roll was the rallying cry. *Animal House* was released in 1977 and I was released in 1978.

For the summer of '79, I was to be employed on the athletic staff at Brown's Hotel in Loch Sheldrake, New York, located in the Catskills—Jerry Lewis's place, according to the ads. A haven for middle- to upper-class Jewish families who liked to eat. There were lots of activities to work off your last meal. I had been there as a guest a few years earlier and hadn't really liked it. Similar to a cruise ship, guests planned the timing of their next meal while they were still eating their prior one. As an employee, however, I thought the hotel would be entertaining.

The Borscht Belt was full of places like Brown's, the Concord, the Nevele, Kutsher's Country Club. Sports, food, entertainment, no dirty dancing between the guests and staff. The waiters made the good bucks. The busboys came in second. At the lowest end of the evolutionary scale was the athletic staff. We had to walk around, look good, supervise guest sporting activities, and set up and break down hotel events. Our pay, if you could call it that, was minimal. We depended upon tips to eke out a living. Unfortunately, we were not invited to many tipping occasions. Accordingly, I believed we had to stand up for our tipping "rights." We were housed two to a room with squeaky single beds and a padlock on the door. There was a community bathroom on each floor in our barracks. Danny, a busboy, and I were assigned the same room. The staff ate together, worked together, and played together. Fraternizing with the guests was discouraged.

When I arrived at Brown's, I brought with me fifteen ounces of fairly good Columbian pot and a zest for life. I decided to stash the pot until I felt comfortable with the Brown's environment and knew the lay of the land. With a razor blade I cut a small straight line in the back of my pillow, carefully placing the pot in individual ounce bags into the middle of the foam and watched the foam close up like a surgical incision that had healed. I then covered the pillow with the pillow case. All secure. The staff didn't get maid service, so no need to worry.

For six weeks at Brown's I had a hell of a time. I worked, partied and bedded a number of pretty coworkers, and made a bunch of good friends among the staff. Slim, a six-foot-eight African American comember of the athletic staff, and I became really close. He had worked at Brown's the summer before and knew everybody. When we weren't smoking pot together, he was teaching me the dos and don'ts of Brown's and who was "cool" and who was not. On one occasion, Slim turned to me with a grin and asked, "Do you know my favorite kind of meal?" Before I could answer, he said, "The free ones." Now he had to show me how it was done.

We drove to the all-night A&P in Liberty, New York, fifteen minutes from Brown's. Slim walked down aisle 1 where the refrigerated cold cuts were and said, "Let's see what's good here today." He asked me whether I preferred ham or salami. "Will that be accompanied by Swiss or American cheese?" he asked. Now carrying the package of ham and Swiss, we made our way to aisle 3 which housed the condiments. "I am in the mood for some Gray Poupon, how about you?" I nodded my head, along for the ride. Based upon Slim's prior shopping experience he knew that the Levy's rye was the best bread for the buck, so that was our next stop. Now it was time to make our sandwiches. We used our fingers to spread the mustard and before you knew it we were walking around the store eating our sandwiches. When our window, I mean aisle, shopping came to an end, our sandwiches had been devoured and we headed for the check out. We each calmly bought a soda, paid, and departed.

Slim ultimately filled me in about Roger, the hotel manager, whom I had met once: a tough guy with a shaved head and a Fu Manchu mustache, who had been a sergeant in Vietnam. He had a nasty reputation. I also learned about the hotel night security staff, manned by the sheriff of Sullivan County on a moonlighting basis.

Other than my occasional sale of a quarter- or half-ounce bag of weed, I generally kept my nose clean. I conducted softball, basketball, shuffleboard, and water polo tournaments and games for the guests. I ran errands for guests and management. And I was ultimately asked to run the spotlights in Brown's nightclub, where the sheriff was a regular. Wearing a headset in the AV room, which was like a small attic with an opening to peer from, I looked over the nightclub to the stage and received my directions from the stage manager. The girls loved my view and often accompanied me to my perch.

Everything seemed to be going along fine, even if I wasn't making much money. I was carefree, stress-free, and along for the ride. That changed quickly. "Roger wants to see you," Slim said with a look of regret. I was summoned to appear before Roger. Roger could intimidate most, and I was no exception. Rumors had swirled that during some unidentified confrontation, Roger had driven a fork through an opponent's hand, wedging it to a table top. His large physique, piercing eyes and clean-shaven head spoke wonders. Roger didn't waste any words and he got right to the point. "I understand you're stirring up trouble." So much for the civilities, I thought.

"What do you mean?"

"I've been told that you're not happy here. You've been complaining."

"I wasn't complaining. Four of us set up the night club for a wedding. The maître d' got a five hundred dollar tip and we got nothing. So I suggested to the guys that we jointly approach Sol and respectfully ask for a piece of the tip. That was it."

"It's really simple. You have two choices. You can stay here and shut the fuck up. Stop causing trouble and do your job. Or you can leave." So much for the training in social etiquette.

I thought for a moment but not too long. "Well, the bottom line is if I think I'm being mistreated I'm going to say something."

"I want you off the property in thirty minutes. Do you understand?" Roger responded.

I nodded.

As easy as that my employment at Brown's ended. I walked from Roger's office feeling completely shell-shocked.

I passed Ralph, one of my coworkers, a young Puerto Rican kid, and told him I had been canned. He couldn't believe it. For that matter, neither could I.

I wasn't thrilled about the prospect of saying goodbye to all the friends I had made. As I walked across the grounds of Brown's, I contemplated my next move.

At the staff housing quarters, a barracks of sorts, I made my way back to my room. Padlock after padlock on each door. A strange symmetry. From a distance down the hallway I could see that my room door was open, and I figured that my roommate Danny must have been inside.

My heart began to race as I approached. The combination lock and metal bracket had been ripped off the door and remained affixed to but dangling from the door jam. Our space had been invaded. Clothing was strewn about the floors. The chests of drawers on both sides of the room had been emptied, with the drawers housing our possessions flipped onto the floor. The beds had been stripped, sheets and pillow cases thrown about. Our toiletry cases had been emptied. Suitcases and duffel bags, which had been securely snug under the beds, were now in plain view. The place was a shambles. A discordant noise was ringing in my head as my body pulsated in anticipation of what might happen next. Everything went silent and the naked pillow stared at me from atop the mattress.

I was short of breath but knew what I had to do. I turned the pillow over and separated the foam with one hand, reaching inside with the other. My eyes were closed for a half second and I was waiting to hear someone say, "You're under arrest" with cuffs closing on my wrists, but there was silence. I reached into the pillow and pulled out the three and a half ounces of remaining pot.

They hadn't found what they were looking for. It was clearly time for me to leave. I threw all of my belongings into my duffel bag and ran to my car with my possessions. I drove the four-and-a-half-hour trip straight to Boston and didn't regain my composure till I had crossed the Massachusetts state line.

I arrived in Boston with no job, no place to sleep, and virtually no money. During my trip to Massachusetts, I adopted the song "Ain't No Stopping Us Now," by McFadden and Whitehead, as my new theme song. My first night in town, I slept in the back seat of my car. I was down but not out. Over the next week, I found a job as a painter/utility man on the Brandeis campus and rented a one-bedroom apartment in Brighton. Life went on.

15.
Gamblers Anonymous

Monday through Saturday had been profitable. Getting up at six a.m. each morning and studying the hoop point spreads had paid off. I was up some big bucks and was primed to break the bank. Of course, with Sunday upon me, I couldn't resist going for broke. I bet thirteen games, three hundred dollars on each and lost twelve of them with the vig (the bookie's 10 percent commission on a loss). I was down 3,690 dollars for the day, 2,920 dollars for the week. I couldn't believe it. I questioned my judgment and was angry at myself.

I walked into the meeting a complete ingénue. I had called the Gamblers Anonymous hotline at 11:45 on Sunday night, a not uncommon time for first-time callers. Nineteen and carefree, but with certain demons in my midst, my thirteen sure bets on Sunday had failed to fulfill my prophecy. Going for the "kill" hadn't worked. "Big Gus" would be paying me a visit to collect. If you can let yourself down, I had, and I didn't know what to do or which way to turn. I called Gamblers Anonymous. Pat was manning the hotline. An amicable sort, we spoke for twenty-five minutes or so. He sounded inspired, rattling off the virtues of GA like he was reciting the alphabet. Recognizing your addiction was the first step. A confidential peer group would provide positive reinforcement that could help change your life. "You called. The first step was done. You knew you weren't in control. Come to the meeting. It will help you." How could I say no?

The Knights of Columbus Hall in Newton, Massachusetts, was filled with sixth-grade cafeteria-style tables and chairs. A few bulletin board posters were on the wall, but otherwise the room was cold and stark. Coffee and donuts were sitting on a counter. Acquaintances were making small talk to pass the time before the meeting started. People who didn't want to be, but needed to be, were there. Whether for themselves or their loved ones, they were committed. (Some certainly should have been committed...) Copies of the Gamblers Anonymous handbook were meticulously placed at consistent intervals around the long rectangular table. The bible. Like Alcoholics Anonymous, the guiding principles were clear in a twelve-step program.

1. You had to admit you were "powerless" over gambling and that your life had become unmanageable due to it.

2. You needed to acknowledge that a power greater than yourself could help restore you to a normal life.

3. You had to subvert your will and life to this "power."

4. You had to look within and take an inventory of yourself.

5. You had to admit to yourself and others that you were a compulsive gambler and the nature of your wrongs.

6. You had to be ready to accept and work at changing the defects in your character.

7. You had to "humbly" ask God for assistance in removing your defects.

8. & 9. You were required to make a list of those you hurt and how you would make amends to them.

10. You needed to commit to continue to take personal inventory of yourself and admit when you were wrong.

11. You had to engage in prayer and meditation to improve your relationship with God and self-knowledge; and

12. You needed to spread these principles to other compulsive gamblers in need of help.

I looked around the room and thought of Sky Masterson in *Guys and Dolls*, played by Marlon Brando, bringing twenty sinners to Sister Sarah's prayer meeting. Wondering who could play me.

Pat had accurately described himself to me over the phone two nights earlier and it was not difficult to find the two-hundred-and-thirty-pound man with a beard and a smile. My sponsor sat next to me and tried to make me feel at home with his warm disposition. He had an uphill battle. He didn't tell me much about himself, but it was clear he was in his mid-forties, and our conversation revealed he was married with children and responsibilities. I compared my life with his and we had little in common, except the "bet." I was nineteen and carefree and he wasn't.

As the other members of this dysfunctional support group entered the room, I realized I was half the age of my nearest counterpart. A scary looking lot, I studied their faces as they found their respective seats. As a betting man, I would have wagered that they took precisely the same seat from meeting to meeting, leaving the same seat open for the newbie, which this week was me. Hardened and weary looks were obvious: The forty-year-old blonde looked fifty-five, washed out and weathered from too much of the good life; the house painter in his work jeans, spattered clothing, parched face; the security guard still in his Wackenhut uniform, dreary, tired, sad; the gray-haired woman with the red "Friendly's" logo on her white dress, peppered with ketchup, mustard and grease stains. All were there, accepting the cards that were dealt, and resigned to an insignificant future, dealing with the devil within.

As the lone new attendee, I was asked to speak first. Initially, I was self-conscious, but after a moment I got on a roll, like playing backgammon for hours until I couldn't focus. "Hello, my name is Brian and I'm a compulsive gambler." Nobody in the room cared why. They just wanted me to say I knew I was one of them. A red badge of courage. A Blood. A Crip. An equal. As a newcomer, it was my job to tell the story of how I got there. Anecdotally, I recalled my first real bet, and then rattled off a number of gambling experiences:

Playing poker and blackjack with my childhood friends for baseball cards, coins, comic books, and the like. Moving on to betting obsidian, pyrite, and galena from my geology collection—getting my rocks off.

Betting on a blind gerbil racing a seeing gerbil down a corridor.

Wagering on whether an M-80 could blow out all four glass panels of a stationary telephone booth in Greenwich Village.

As I told my stories most of the dispassionate men and women around the table broke out in laughter. Enjoying the attention, I piled on. Playing scopa in Napoli, Italy, at age twelve with older men, using a pile of Lira that wasn't mine.

Playing pot-limit poker with eighteen year olds at the Saint Luke's afterschool center on Hudson Street, where none of the nuns knew what was going on.

Betting on Vanderbilt getting two-and-a-half points from Duke in a college football game. Vanderbilt is winning 28-0 at halftime. The boys and I are counting our winnings. We play two-hand touch football in the schoolyard and check the score two hours later. Duke wins 31-28. We lose. Stupefied we each look at each other and say okay, whose car are we going to take to the Verrazano Bridge and who is jumping first?

I told them about my best friend when I was seventeen who was Italian, and that we went to church together on Sundays and he sought guidance on which NFL team to take Sunday afternoon. When our Saturday college football forecasts had not been achieved, he asked God, "Why?" He studied hard and was responsible in school, but gambling was gambling. He deserved to find inspiration in church before making his Sunday selections. If he didn't deserve divine intervention, who did? Of course, if all else failed and we were really desperate for a winner, I talked about the pick of the day, the pick of the week, the pick of the month. I talked about "lock" picks, the ones you couldn't lose. I talked about streaks, mostly losing ones. Everyone in the room could relate to the term "lock bet," and other catch phrases and experiences.

Through the stories, people in the room could relate to me. They understood; nothing needed to be explained. Heads nodded. Muffled comments under their breath.

When I wrapped up my presentation, a feeling of accomplishment came over me. I had taken the first step, acknowledging that I had a problem. Now I could get the hell out of there, or so I thought.

Now it was their turn. Each of the attendees was given some time to speak.

"Hi, I'm Bob, I'm a compulsive gambler. GA has been good for me. I haven't bet in twenty-three months."

"Hi, I'm Sarah. I'm a compulsive gambler. Before joining Gamblers Anonymous my life was in a shambles. I couldn't keep a job, my marriage was on the rocks. GA was the first step in getting my life back in order."

When the third speaker rose, he didn't immediately talk but instead slowly looked at all the faces in the room, one by one. After thirty to forty-five seconds of silence that seemed like an eternity, the unshaven man with Peter Lorre beady eyes and an unhealthy jaundiced complexion, looked directly at me.

"My name is Joe. I am a compulsive gambler. I have not gambled in over four years." He paused and gestured toward me. "That young man made you all laugh. It is wrong to laugh."

He just stood there staring directly at me. A lump formed in my throat. Then he sat down. After two more participants made their pledges of allegiance, a small man with a raspy voice stood to make his plea.

"My name is Kevin. I am a compulsive gambler. Gamblers Anonymous has helped me quit gambling. I haven't had any action for over seven years. Last week I robbed a liquor store with two other guys. When we walked in a mother and her two children were by the cash register. As I screamed for everyone to stand still and be quiet, I would have shot anybody in the store who didn't listen: the mother, the children, the storekeeper. I didn't care. We left the store with a bunch of money and I kept it all. They know they will have to kill me to get any of it."

The tension in the room was remarkable. Nobody said a word. Kevin drifted back to us.

"Well, anyway, Gamblers Anonymous has been great for me. I haven't gambled in seven years." I looked at my sponsor in disbelief, but he was in denial. GA was a place to deal with gambling addictions, but its membership turned a deaf ear to other social transgressions. You were there for one purpose and one purpose only.

I left the room knowing I would never be back.

16.
Flashback 1971—
Ciro and a Little Taste of Italy

My mother met Ciro C. in Little Italy in New York City in 1971 during a rainy night when each was hailing a yellow cab and got in simultaneously on opposite sides. What could have been the start of an improbable Hollywood love story became a truly exhilarating but rocky romance for my mom.

Ciro was from Napoli, Italy, a stout man with rugged good looks, a big head of curly hair, demonstrative sideburns and an authoritative voice, although he spoke only *poco-poco* ("a little") English. He was strong and charming and just the man to sweep my mother off her feet, which were not too firmly planted on the ground to begin with.

With Ciro, money was no object. Fancy meals, then dresses, diamonds, emeralds, and fur coats soon adorned Mom. Ciro was a man of mystery and intrigue. His front, an import-export business with no name. His "get out of jail free card," a photo in his wallet of Lucky Luciano and Ciro hugging at the airport in Napoli in the late 1950s, years after Luciano's luck in the United States had ended and he was deported back to Italy.

Italian restaurant owners in New York greeted Ciro when he arrived to taste their cuisine, many embracing him cheek-to-cheek. When the *Godfather* had its premiere in 1972 at the Ziegfeld Theatre in New York City, my mother and Ciro had eighth-row center seats.

Ciro took us to Naples during the summers of 1971 and 1972. He and my mother lived in Naples, while my sister and I lived with Maria, Ciro's sister and her large family of nine children in a home in a seaside village called Torregoveta. My days were spent on the beach, swimming, fishing, and playing Italian football (our soccer). Once a week or so Ciro would say, "Tonight I take out the boy." Invariably Ciro alone would pick me up in a red Ferrari or on a Harley Davidson motorcycle, which were at his disposal, and we would go to dinner, then to a speakeasy/men's club with drinking and gambling. I would be given stacks of lira bills to gamble with and to play "scopa," an Italian card game, and coins to play pinball. As an eleven- and twelve-year old, I was in heaven.

Late in 1972, there was a sharp knock at our apartment door in Manhattan on West 16th Street in the middle of the night. Federal authorities with an arrest warrant entered our home and led Ciro away in handcuffs. We were not even apprised of the charges and my mother became hysterical.

A few days later my mother received a phone call from someone in Italy advising her to go to the Alitalia terminal at Kennedy Airport and await the arrival of a particular plane. The messenger was to know what my mother looked like so there would be no "problems." I was asked to accompany my mom to the airport. After the plane arrived, a well-dressed man with slicked backed hair, wearing dark sunglasses, approached my mother and me. He reached into his carry-on strapped shoulder bag and pulled out a folded large manila envelope that was thick and taped shut. He said *buongiorno*, handed my mother the envelope, then said, *ciao* and was gone. It was never clear to me if the twenty-five thousand dollars was used for bail or to hire an attorney. Following Ciro's release from jail, he was deported and never returned to the United States. His karma, to follow in the steps of Lucky Luciano, his patron saint.

During a short drug-induced epiphany in college I wrote Ciro to tell him that I missed him and frequently thought about the good times we had had together during the 1970s. I suggested that as a parental figure he had a positive influence on me.

I received back a letter from Blundeston Prison located in the village of Blundeston in Suffolk, England, marked "censored mail." Apparently, my letter was forwarded there. The responsive letter, translated by Ciro's cellmate, thanked me for my correspondence, but suggested that I not use Ciro as a role model. Wise advice. Given the option, prison was no place I wanted to call "home." That was my last communication with Ciro.

17.
The Art of Middling

Middling is a gambling device for degenerate gamblers who are fortunate enough to have two bookies at their disposal instead of one. On Wall Street, arbitragers buy commodities in one territory and resell in another, making a profit on the price differential that may exist between the two. The gamblers' closest connection to arbitrage is middling. You can't middle in most sports, but you can in basketball. Middling is betting on an underdog in a game getting points with one bookie and betting on the favorite on the same game giving points with another bookie. You can only middle if there is a disparity in the point line between the two bookies. For example, if the Celtics were playing the Knicks in Boston and one bookie had the Celtics favored by four and another had the Celtics favored by two, a middle would be betting five hundred dollars on the Celtics giving two points with one bookie and taking the Knicks getting four points from the other also for a five hundred dollar wager. If the Celtics win by two, three, or four points you are in the money, winning five hundred dollars, one thousand dollars, or five hundred dollars respectively. If any other result takes place you win one bet, lose the other and lose the vigorish, which is ten percent of your wager. Many factors affect a point spread, including where the bookie is located, who his clients are, and who they are fans of.

In college I mastered the art of the middle and won a decent chunk of change in the process. The risks were minimal as long as both bookies you used were reliable in paying their debts if you won.

18.
The Outer Limits—
College Daze, Women,
Gambling, Petty Crime

When you just don't care, you can do some really stupid things. In 1981, with graduation from college still not a reality, I reached the depths of debauchery. I was dealing drugs to support my gambling habit, and indiscriminately sleeping with anybody I could get into bed. I hosted poker games and all-night backgammon matches with other compulsive gamblers. Each morning I bought the *Boston Globe*, tore out the sports lines with the spreads and studied them in class to determine the bets of the day. I was selling two to three pounds of pot a week, and numb to life. For an occasional thrill, I would drive my 1974 Grand Prix with a powerful 400 4-barrel engine in front of the campus security station, peel out, leaving tread marks. A campus security officer would then chase me down on the campus artery drive and give me an eight-dollar ticket for my joy ride. It was the best eight-dollar adventure I knew.

Consistent with my attitude toward life, my two favorite songs were "Life in The Fast Lane" and "Born to Be Wild."

I drank to excess and was not a nice person. On one particularly sordid night, I drove to IHOP with my buddy hoping that some food would reduce my drunken state. We "chewed and screwed" without paying the tab. Next, we went to campus and at two in the morning pilfered an ugly couch from the fifth floor of a dorm, coming back an hour later to take the matching ugly love seat. Rumors swirled that members of the Brandeis soccer team had to have done the daring deed. Ironically, one of the campus security guards named Dougie, with whom I was friends, asked me if I had heard through the grape-vine who had done the theft. I calmly told him that only the guys from the Brandeis soccer team had the balls to do that one.

A few months later I had a date with a very nice girl from Bran-deis. We went back to my apartment after the date and were sitting on the edge of my waterbed having a drink when she spotted the ugly loveseat. The mood abruptly changed as she asked me where I got it. I told her the back of a truck, but didn't think she believed me. She left in a huff, telling me that she and five suitemates had chipped in to buy the couch and loveseat. Just my luck. Not the best way to finish a date.

My socially redeemable qualities had hit an all-time low and my future looked bleak. I had no goals or aspirations and was simply living for the moment. Some people never grow up. Some people never get a second chance.

Sometimes new leases on life are arrived at by processes that are arbitrary and not subject to logical explanation.

19.
Mescaline and the LSAT

It was during my final year of college that it dawned on me to take the LSAT as a lark. Law school might save me from an ignominious life. If the drugs, gambling, and other assorted anti-social behavior didn't do me in, I had a chance. My father had gone back to law school later in life as a third or fourth career, and had become a lawyer. However, he was not my role model, having flown the coop and divorced my mother when I was ten, and I didn't wish anybody to perceive that I was following in his footsteps. If somebody were to comment that the apple didn't fall far from the tree, I was quick to say that I was from a different orchard.

Law school was an amorphous concept when I was twenty and I approached it like most other things: with reckless abandon. Those who had a true desire to attend law school took the Stanley Kaplan LSAT (Law School Aptitude Test) prep course to hone their analytical abilities and adjust their thought processes to respond to the sophisticated questions posed by standardized tests and the people that draft them.

As a successful drug dealer, gambler, and womanizer who had played varsity lacrosse and run track, I certainly did not need to devote any precious time to a silly review class.

In the six months leading up to the LSAT, I spent approximately four hours perusing some materials for the test. When the big day came, I was ready. The test was given on a Saturday morning in Boston. The day before, I purchased my four lead pencils, the number two variety, and four tabs of mescaline. Friday afternoon I called Virginia from Bentley College, an attractive although a bit vapid Italian girl who served as an occasional playmate. By eight p.m., Virginia was at my apartment. We each took two hits (tabs) of mescaline. A cloud had engulfed my mind and body. By 9:30 we were both naked in front of my fireplace, giggling. The flames were dancing to a magnificent melody that only we could hear. The trials and tribulations of life were not before us. We had each other for this fleeting time. We laughed and laughed ultimately slumping in exhaustion in each other's arms curled up together in a blanket as the last log in the fireplace burned out. I woke up Saturday morning at six to the sound of my alarm clock blaring in my room. My head was in a total fog, a cloud still engulfed me. After suffering through a shower, I located the directions to the test site, collected my pencils, and drove to Boston. Virginia was still asleep in my living room. Everybody at the LSAT test center looked bright-eyed and bushy-tailed, but somewhat anxious. I was too wiped out to be nervous. Dragging ass, I looked at my peers. Their faces revealed that they believed their lives and careers depended on the outcome of this test; it was a life test. The LSAT of course didn't measure whether you were good or bad, moral or immoral, sensitive, empathetic or kind. The LSAT wouldn't even tell you if law school was for you or not. The proctors ushered everybody to their seats, explained the rules and let us all know we would be under their watchful eyes. All I wanted to do was to go back to sleep. Luckily, I was one of those people who excel on standardized tests.

I still wondered aloud what the hell I was doing there. The test taker with whom I shared a table thought I was talking to myself. I was. Finally, the test booklets were passed out facedown. It was the moment of truth or consequences. I closed my eyes for a second of contemplation. I vaguely recall hearing a proctor say that the test had now begun. I needed a moment or two to regroup. My mind was elsewhere. Where, I wasn't sure. After a few minutes, I opened my eyes and looked around at my zealous colleagues intently analyzing the crossword puzzles before them. As my hooded eyes wandered around the room, one of the proctors glanced at me with disdain as if I was misbehaving. That was my cue. I had given all my competitors a few minutes head start. They were all tortoises and I was the hare. Neither the test itself nor my results were noteworthy. I remember finishing the test in thirty-five minutes before our allotted time. After handing in my test booklet I walked over to the proctor whose gaze had got me going. I broke the four number two pencils in half, handed him the eight broken pencil halves and said, "Now I'm free." All in a day's work.

TURNING TO
A STRAIGHT AND
NARROW PATH

20.
The Fork in the Road

"When you get to the fork in the road, take it."
—Attributed to Yogi Berra

Similar to the life of a lawsuit, where there are specific pressure-point opportunities to reach a settlement prior to a new phase of combat, one's life has a limited number of critical junctures where significant forks in the road present themselves. My fork in the road came when I was twenty, on my way to graduating college with no responsibilities or commitments and a history of depraved indifference. My sports activities and drug dealing had made me socially popular in a superficial way. I was generally at the center of attention, but for the wrong reasons. I didn't care about anybody or myself. With no discipline or moral compass, I embarked on one meaningless joyride after another. You can't, however, be a party animal forever. All play and no work makes Jack a dull boy. Ultimately, in order to gain the respect of your peers, you need to lead by example. In college, I was not a good example.

As a result of not being connected to either of my parents, I more often than not made my own decisions with little input from others, even if, up to that point, most of my decisions were poor ones. Somehow life lets you draw straws to determine whether you are destined to be a leader or a follower. While I had had no role models, I drew from the first pile. I didn't want to join the Peace Corps and save the world, but I wanted to make a difference and leave my mark, however that would come about.

I couldn't be a drug dealing, gambling, womanizer for my entire life.

There was an irony that I attended Brandeis in the first instance as it was a nonsectarian, primarily Jewish school established in 1948 in tribute to Supreme Court Justice Louis Brandeis who served on the bench from 1916 to 1931. The student body was primarily made up of upper-middle-class, intelligent, articulate and competitive individuals, many of whom were seeking to distinguish themselves from the pack. Slackers did not last long at Brandeis.

I had learned how to juggle my business, my passions, my compulsions, and my classes. My peers and my very capable professors had helped push me scholastically, and I learned how to succinctly express my opinions in a reasoned manner, a good preparation for law school that was on the horizon, unbeknownst to me.

Leading up to my graduation from Brandeis in May of 1982, the fork in the road for my life had two prongs: Join the army as a second lieutenant or go to law school if there was a law school that would have me. Either prong would have involved discipline, one inflicted upon me and the other self-invoked to succeed.

Going backpacking through Western Europe for three months following my graduation from Brandeis, I postponed my fate. I had conferred with an army recruiter in Waltham, Massachusetts, and was ready, willing, and able to enlist in September. The army was looking for "a few good men," as they had been for generations, and I could surely fit the bill. I was healthy enough to endure basic training and could follow orders if I had to. The problem with the army was that I would be required to adhere to archaic rules, be subject to rote drills, and would be a subordinate to many individuals with significantly less intellectual curiosity than I. It beat going to jail as a drug dealer, but not by a lot.

Then there was the law school route. Notwithstanding my mescaline experiment the night before the LSAT, I scored in the fifty-fifth percentile. That, combined with my GPA between a B and B+, gave me a shot at a few institutions. I applied to four marginal law schools, was rejected by one and waitlisted by the other three when my trip abroad started in early June. Unsure of my future, my European adventure, with no strings attached, was my last shebang. Paris, Monte Carlo, the French Riviera, Florence, Rome, and the Greek isle of Corfu. Beautiful cities and beautiful women. What could be wrong? When I got to Venice with a woman on each arm, the Italian men would say, "Perché due?" ("Why two?") and I responded, "Abbondanza" ("Abundance"). Life was good and simple. On my travel through Rome that all changed, and I was forced to be an adult. It was late July and a telex awaited me at the American Express offices in Rome. I had been accepted into law school and school started in less than a month.

Within ten days I received news that I had been accepted to two more schools, three in all, Pace in White Plains, New York, and Suffolk University Law School and New England Law, each of which are in Boston. If I stayed in Boston, I would continue to deal drugs as the money was easy and the supply and demand were both there and I would continue to gamble with bookies and the boyz with whom I had access. A new and responsible life on my way to becoming an attorney meant I had to leave these vices behind. New York was my only sensible choice if I really wanted to grow up and make something of myself. Here was my second chance, an opportunity not necessarily deserved, but here it was.

I wrapped up my European excursions over the next three weeks and headed back to the States to move from Massachusetts back to New York. Law school was going to be like a serious job for me, a foundation to build upon. Following Yogi's advice, I came to a fork in the road, and took it.

My marijuana supplier lived in Newton, Massachusetts. I burned his number. A fitting tribute: "up in smoke." My bookie lived in

Lexington. I couldn't afford the long-distance calls and he was too far away for weekly exchanges of money. (This was before PayPal of course.) Two long-term vices eliminated in a heartbeat.

Law school allowed no time for fun and games. Students ranged from twenty to forty-five and treated studying like a job. With the Socratic method employed in the classrooms nobody wanted to be unprepared or embarrassed when responding to a professor's query.

If you had to reread three times a twenty-four-page Constitutional Law case decision to understand its import, you did it. You formed study groups, you spent time in the law library, you read and then you read some more.

There was now a goal and with a strong will, hard work, and few distractions, it was clear. It was mine for the taking.

I graduated within two-and-a-half years, instead of three years. I finished in the top twelve or thirteen percent of the class and gained confidence that I could make it in the real world. I ultimately learned from the admissions department of Pace that I was the last person selected for admission off the waiting list during the summer of 1982. I had matured during my time in law school and was more introspective and mindful of how I treated others. They took a chance on me and it paid off for both of us. During law school I didn't gamble, deal drugs, or engage in indiscriminate sexual encounters. I rechanneled my energies to more socially useful functions. I certainly wasn't perfect, but I was "new and improved."

Attending mass in a Catholic church during my senior year in high school, followed by sporadic visits to church while in college, gave me the start of a morality base. After my admission to law school, I became more spiritual and believed that God must have been watching out for me, to give me a second chance. I attended Sunday services throughout my first year of law school and one day went to Father Gregory to inquire about the possibility of converting. He took me to his friary of Franciscan Jesuits and we ate a good meal in a celebratory atmosphere with a lot of red wine. I told Father Gregory what church tenets I believed in and those I didn't. He said I passed the "test" and should be a catechumen with Sister Theresa for six months, studying the bible. Nine months later, I officially converted to Catholicism in 1983, by being baptized in front of a large congregation of parishioners. Religion would ultimately make me more mindful of my conduct toward others and a better person.

21.
Pride Kills

Criminal Law 101, taught by Professor Lowry, was an entertaining class in law school. One particular story he told us left me with an indelible memory.

As a young public defender, Mr. Lowry was called upon to represent a man charged with second-degree murder for killing another man at a Kentucky Fried Chicken fast-food restaurant in Westchester County, New York.

During the initial client interview, Mr. Gonzales, a five foot three Mexican day laborer, confined to the White Plains Detention Center, calmly explained his predicament. While standing on line at the KFC with his girlfriend, a six foot tall African American gentleman cut in front of the two of them. In defense of his dignity he gingerly tapped the line cutter on the back and asked him to move to his proper place in line. Unconvinced that he had committed any transgression and not intimidated by this little man, he refused to budge and barely paid any attention to our five foot three protagonist. The second request by Mr. Gonzales, in broken English, was met with a bit of agitation and some hand flailing, as if trying to get rid of a mosquito. Unfazed by his lack of success, Mr. Gonzales gave it one last college try to remove the impediment from his path to a bucket of extra crispy that he would be taking back to his casa. In a raised voice he now demanded that the man who paid him and his girlfriend no respect move off the line. Having lost his patience, the black man turned to confront Mr. Gonzales and told him to "shut the fuck up" and to leave him alone before he squashes him into the ground. Considering the matter over, he turns back to resume his place in line facing forward. Mr. Gonzales reaches into his pocket and pulls out his work knife. Before he could respond to his assailant, the six foot victim had been stabbed in the back three times. With Mr. Gonzales in a blind rage, he continued to plunge his five-inch blade into his prey.

Mr. Lowry waited for his client to finish recounting the incident, gazed at the little man before him and calmly noted that the deceased in fact was stabbed eighteen times. Mr. Gonzales responded, "Mr. Lowry, wouldn't you have done the same thing?"

22

My First Break as an Attorney

Sometimes being at the right place at the right time is more important than having an encyclopedia's worth of knowledge stored in your head. So it was with my first job out of law school in early 1985. The firm was called Parcher Arisohn & Hayes. Its client roster included the Rolling Stones, Diana Ross, Bruce Springsteen, Paul Simon, John Cougar Mellencamp, and many other notable figures. Through Parcher Arisohn & Hayes I got my first break in the entertainment industry, learned the ropes, and made lifelong connections. When I joined the firm as an associate, I was one of only seven lawyers there, each of whom had client contact and worked on interesting and entertaining matters. Over my five years at the Parcher firm I met and was given access to the players in the industry: lawyers, accountants, personal managers, business managers, and the talent themselves. As a group we worked on a diverse array of cases: copyright and trademark infringement, breach of contract, royalty disputes, and defamation. The experiences I had at Parcher Arisohn & Hayes formed the backbone of my career as an attorney. I was one lucky guy. Mark Arisohn, the attorney who was responsible for bringing me into the firm, nourished me with lessons of humanity, dignity, and integrity. I was a fifteen-year-old boy living in the body of a twenty-four-year-old when Mark took me under his wing.

Mark was my mentor and confidante. He helped teach me right from wrong at a time in my life when most people had already learned it. I saw dignified confidence without chest-beating bravado.

Over time Mark taught me:

- How to analyze a case;
- How to present cogent and forceful legal arguments;
- How to examine a hostile witness; and
- How to instill in a client an understanding that they were safer in my hands than anywhere else.

When I made my seventy-second mistake picking a woman to date, Mark, the "old sage," calmly told me "there will be a seventy-third."

Little did I know at the time, but besides growing as a lawyer from 1985 to 1990, I was growing as a man.

23.
Defending an A-1 Felony Charge

The year was 1986. I had been out of law school for a year and a half and was still an unseasoned attorney. Peter Parcher, the head partner in my small, seven-person law firm, called me into his office. I was being assigned to the case of Richard Diaz, a nineteen-year-old kid from Bayamon, Puerto Rico, who was charged with A-1 felony possession of six-and-a-half ounces of crack cocaine with intent to sell, and automatic weapons. We were to be local counsel for a celebrity mob criminal defense lawyer from Providence, Rhode Island. Since our Rhode Island counsel was not admitted to practice law in New York, I was asked to attend the arraignment and file a notice of appearance as the "attorney of record" on the case. Little did I know that our primary counsel would only remain in the picture a few weeks, never to be heard from again.

Richard spoke no English, and I spoke no Spanish. Through the aid of an interpreter I was able to meet with him briefly before the arraignment and learn that he claimed his innocence. Richard was a fence mender in Bayamon, visiting his cousin in New York on a seven-day vacation paid for by his mother. He had never left Puerto Rico before. The criminal court complaint indicated that Richard was charged with drug and weapons possession.

Based upon the severity of the criminal charges, Richard's lack of community contacts and his "risk" of flight, his bail was set at one hundred thousand dollars, a sum that a nineteen-year-old *non*-drug dealer cannot raise. Richard was ordered to be held at Rikers Island, a high-security facility not for the faint of heart. Rikers Island is one of the world's largest correctional institutions, housing over eleven thousand inmates and often ranked within the ten worst prisons in the United States.

My last communication with Rhode Island counsel was a short conversation where I was given the phone number for Richard's grandmother and asked to get a complete factual debriefing from Richard.

Nobody told me that I could have submitted certain paperwork to the court to have Richard brought from Rikers to the courthouse. Accordingly, for my first full-length meeting with Richard, I arranged to go directly to Rikers. An interpreter was set to meet me there. At Rikers, I was ushered through numerous layers of security until I was told that Richard had not been retrieved from his cell despite the paperwork calling for his retrieval. As it turned out, there were four R. Diaz's within the facility and the authorities had not narrowed down which one was my Richard. I was told that to expedite matters I could walk cell to cell in one of the cell blocks to see if I could find Richard, and I agreed to do so. Dressed in a two-piece suit and carrying a briefcase, I didn't quite fit in with my environs. The walk was unremarkable as I bellowed out "Richard Diaz" repeatedly until I came to a cell with a tattoo-covered muscle-bound man wearing a wife beater t-shirt who was profusely bleeding from a significant gash on his forehead. As the blood streamed down both sides of his face he attempted to wipe the moisture from his eyes. He was leaning on the bars of the cell door peering out when I walked by. This inmate was a scary sight. Our eyes connected for a brief moment, but it was long enough to set him off like a firecracker.

"What the fuck are you looking at?" he said, his voice full of menace.

As I jumped back, startled, a new air of confidence inspired this imprisoned man.

"You fuckin' think I look bad motherfucker? You should see the three guys that were messin' with me."

Enough said. I swiftly moved from my encounter down the cell block. With no luck finding Richard, I went back to the administrative offices from which I had come and was told that my client had been located. I breathed a sigh of relief as I did not want to play another round of truth or consequences walking through the cell blocks.

Richard was five foot three, frail, and unshaven. He soldered fences on farms in southern Puerto Rico to prevent cows from wandering. He was not old enough to drink in New York. On his seven-day vacation to New York, Richard was to stay with his twenty-two-year-old cousin, Elivio, who lived in a tough neighborhood on 157th Street. During their second day together, Richard and Elivio had gone to Kentucky Fried Chicken and brought back food to Elivio's apartment. Each of the four bedrooms in the apartment had padlocks on their respective doors and there was a communal kitchen, bathroom, and living room, with a couch and television for all to use. Elivio's was the first bedroom off the front door to the left. According to Richard, Elivio left the apartment after they had come home, his bedroom door was open and Richard was watching TV and eating chicken in the communal living room, when about forty minutes later, there was a knock at the door. Richard went to the door, asked who it was, and heard Elivio's voice say it was Arnaldo. Hearing Elivio's voice, Richard naively opened the door. Three undercover police officers with guns drawn and Elivio already in handcuffs awaited on the other side. Richard was forced to the ground at gunpoint as two of the officers conducted a warrantless search of the apartment and Elivio's bedroom adjacent to the front door, where drugs and weapons were found hidden away under a bed.

Richard was arrested and charged with an A-1 felony punishable by twenty-five years to life in prison. Elivio was arrested and initially charged with loitering with intent to sell narcotics, a class B misdemeanor. If Richard was telling the truth he was simply at the wrong place at the wrong time, a defense that many a judge would find incredulous.

My defense strategy was simple: make a motion to suppress the evidence claiming that Richard was arrested without "probable" cause and therefore the weapons and drugs found after his liberty was unconstitutionally curtailed were fruits of the poisonous tree (i.e., the illegal arrest) and inadmissible as evidence against him. Since Richard was visiting his cousin, under existing case precedents, he could not claim that the search of the apartment was without probable cause because Richard did not have "a reasonable expectation of privacy" in someone else's home. If we lost our suppression motion, Richard would be in dire straits as it would be his word at trial versus the word of a number of police officers as to how he possessed the contraband.

As the case developed, I obtained through the discovery process the police's version of the events. Elivio had been selling crack cocaine in the street when an undercover agent attempted to apprehend him. Elivio eluded his pursuer, ran into his building and made it back to his apartment with the police in "hot pursuit." When the police knocked on the door Elivio opened it, the police walked into the apartment to arrest Elivio and in so doing saw the drugs and weapons on a table in Elivio's bedroom in "plain view" with Richard hovering and exercising "dominion and control" over the table.

In order to properly cross-examine the police officers, I ventured to 157th Street in Washington Heights to examine Elivio's apartment and the scene of the arrest. I parked my Trans-Am a few blocks from the apartment, hoping it would still be there when I returned. I was wearing a blue button-down shirt but left my suit jacket and tie in the car. When I entered the building, a number of people screamed "policia, policia," and ran in different directions. I felt like I was part of an episode of the cartoon, *Speedy Gonzales*, with everything and everyone moving at breakneck speed.

The lone person left in the lobby was a black gentleman calmly leaning against a wall. He took one look at me and said, "You a lawyer or you a cop?" Before I finished getting the words out of my mouth, he remarked, "You a fucking stupid lawyer to come in here looking like that." I asked where I could find apartment 503 and he pointed me to the stairs.

When I got to the unit on the fifth floor, I knocked and an older unshaven gentleman with a beer in his hand opened the door. He spoke little English but generally understood why I was there and allowed me in. The apartment consisted of four bedrooms, three of them locked with padlocks and an open door for the fourth bedroom belonging to my host. There was a dilapidated and torn grass-green couch in front of a TV set from 1965 with a rabbit ears antenna above in a living room area that apparently everyone shared, along with a kitchen and bathroom. The old man confirmed that Elivio's bedroom, which was locked, was similar in dimensions to his little room. The odds of a drug dealer having significant amounts of crack cocaine and weapons sitting on a small table in the middle of the room, when opening the front door for the police, were slim to none.

There were a number of court appearances leading up to the day of the suppression hearing. I learned that Elivio had 347 dollars on his person when he was arrested and Richard had eleven dollars. The prosecutor had upped the charges on Elivio to the same offenses as Richard. Elivio had prior drug-related convictions and Richard none. Nobody could give a feasible explanation as to why the police only initially charged Elivio with loitering with intent to sell drugs if they saw him selling narcotics then chased him in "hot pursuit" culminating with his arrest in his apartment ten to fifteen feet from the drugs. It didn't add up.

Criminal Court judges in the New York State court system have a difficult job. They generally have huge backlogs of cases and are under constant pressure to move them along to resolution. Frequently, without knowing many pertinent facts, they pressure defendants to take plea bargains. Our judge was no different. Even before the suppression hearing began he, through an interpreter, told Richard that he should accept a plea to a Class B felony, which would carry a sentence of five to twenty-five, where Richard could be released as early as three and a half years later.

As Richard continued to maintain his innocence, the judge constantly badgered him to plead guilty. On one court appearance, Richard arrived with a black eye and swollen cheek, a gift from fellow inmates at Rikers. One had tried to rape him. After three months and seventeen days on the inside, Richard's spirit and body were faltering. It was now December, approaching Christmas, and the streets of New York were bustling with shoppers and anticipation. Richard was in a tiny cell waiting to be judged for a crime he did not commit.

The Special Narcotics Division of the New York District Attorneys' Office was under the auspices of Sterling Johnson. They were in the business of getting results and convictions, ridding the streets of drug dealers. Consistent with their hard-nosed approach, they let you know that if you proceeded with a suppression hearing in an attempt to exercise your client's constitutional rights, making them spend the time to defend against your motion, any plea bargain offer previously put on the table would be removed. Although I had already alerted Richard to this fact, our judge drove home the point hard before the hearing was to start.

Richard started to buckle. The pressure became too much to bear. Through the interpreter, Richard sheepishly told me he wanted to plead guilty to the lesser offense, calculating how old he would be when he got out of prison. Convinced of his innocence and disillusioned by his change in resolve, I told Richard that in order to plead guilty he would need to do an allocution in open court pointing to the drugs and automatic weapons and acknowledging they were his. Richard began to cry and in Spanish said that was something he could not do.

Two police officers and Richard testified during the first day of the suppression hearing; Elivio did not. Elivio's attorney and I each conducted thorough and compelling cross-examinations of the officers and their logic in charging Elivio initially with only loitering, which did not hold up to scrutiny. Richard was convincing even though his testimony directly contradicted that of the police officers. It was uncontroverted that Richard lived in Puerto Rico, was in New York on a vacation, and that the contraband was all discovered in Elivio's room.

Over the course of my representation of Richard his demeanor and persona had significantly changed. Initially he was indignant and combative about his unjust arrest. Following his months of incarceration at Rikers and the browbeating from the judge, he became fatalistic and lost the will to fight for his cause. Now, at the end of our first day of hearing, Richard was seriously depressed. Fearing for Richard's safety, I asked our judge to have him put on a suicide watch. With the stroke of a pen, his shoelaces and belt were confiscated, he was not permitted to shave, and he was checked on more frequently.

Criminal defense attorneys who have many years of experience defending accused criminal defendants learn as a defense mechanism to become detached from their clients, and not get caught up with their potential guilt or innocence. I, on the other hand, was consumed by my representation of Richard, worried that my lack of experience could facilitate an innocent man going to prison for a long time.

Before the second day of the proceeding, the judge called all attorneys into his chambers and told the two ADAs working the case that he believed Richard was innocent and Elivio was guilty, that he would prefer not to rule on the suppression motion, that the government should dismiss its case against Richard and offer a B-Felony plea to Elivio before we went any further. I couldn't believe my ears but did not want to get too excited before anything official happened. The judge also said he would personally call Sterling Johnson and make the recommendation.

Court was temporarily adjourned. Richard and Elivio were returned to their holding cells and the ADAs were busy deciding their next moves. By early afternoon they had their marching orders. They would agree to dismiss their case against Richard subject to Elivio agreeing to the plea suggested by the judge. As soon as I heard this I went into attack mode. How could one man's liberty be deprived based upon another man's decision to do time or not. Constitutional due process was being violated. If the government didn't believe it had a case against Richard then they should just dismiss their case against him. While the judge did not disagree, he was also pragmatic. He instructed Elivio's lawyer to have a long talk with his client. It was 3:45 p.m. when Elivio's attorney came back with the news that his client would accept the plea. By 4:30 p.m. we were on the record in court and Elivio was acknowledging his ownership of the drugs and weapons. His sentencing would be thirty days later.

The judge's clerk prepared the order that I anxiously awaited, a document confirming that the case against Richard was dismissed and directing the warden to release him. The judge handed me the signed order and said, "Good job, counselor. You fought well for your client."

My heart was racing as I carried the order to the lock-up area where Richard was located. I gave the order to an officer and was pointed to his cell. As the officer walked, I ran. I got to the cell and said, "Tue es libre." Richard began to cry and so did I. The weight was lifted off my chest as the cell door opened and Richard hugged me sobbing. It was the most rewarding day in court I ever had even though we weren't paid a penny for my time.

LIFE AS AN ENTERTAINMENT LAWYER

24.
Rodney Dangerfield—
No Respect

The year was 1986, and Rodney Dangerfield was at the apex of his career. *Back to School* had propelled Rodney's popularity across a large swatch of America, and he was recognized wherever he roamed. I was a second-year lawyer assigned to represent Rodney in a case he had against the NBC television network relating to NBC's failure to air during the 1984 Super Bowl half-time show a fifteen-minute filmed skit produced, funded by, and starring Rodney. NBC at the behest of Bob Costas, a huge Rodney fan, had agreed in writing that if they approved the script they would air the show at half-time of the Bears-Patriots game. When Rodney was done, the final edited production did not meet NBC's approval, although they had no "approval rights." Before my involvement in the matter, as a compromise in court, NBC agreed to air the skit during its pregame show before billions less people, and Rodney was allowed to continue his suit for the difference in value between the two airings, the pregame show audience versus the half-time show audience.

Rodney's deposition was scheduled for a Thursday, and his prep was the day before. He sauntered into my office in his inimical cavalier style and grimaced, "So what do I have to know for this thing tomorrow?" Two hours and twenty-seven distractions later, Rodney was ready to go. To the extent anybody could prepare Rodney Dangerfield for a deposition, I had done so. He had made a point of saying to every woman under forty-five in my office, "Hey babe, if I was a little bit younger, I would be coming on to you right now."

Dangerfield insisted that I pick him up at his apartment on East

66th Street. When I arrived, dressed in a three-piece suit and carrying my attaché case, another man let me into the apartment. There was Rodney, wearing his boxer shorts and an undershirt and walking on a treadmill. He hollered to me, "Hey, Bri, come over, tell me a few jokes and loosen me up. I'm a bit nervous for this deposition thing."

I walked across the room and stood next to him as he labored half-dressed on his apparatus, sweating profusely. Before long I was cajoled to tell a few jokes. Incredibly, the third one hit. An offshoot of "Big Jule" in *Guys and Dolls* where he brags about his clean criminal record reflected by eighteen arrests and not one conviction. Rodney broke stride, laughed and stumbled, almost falling off the treadmill. As he reached to turn off the machine, Rodney quipped, "Hey I might use that in my next movie." I responded, "Will you give me credit?"

Rodney smiled his devilish smile and quipped, "Yeah, kid, thanks."

The double stretch limo that waited for us was farcical in nature, a comedic car for a comedian. The driver was in a different zip code. We drove to Maiden Lane in lower Manhattan in the Wall Street area, a very narrow cobblestone paved street. When we pulled up to the office building, which housed Cahill Gordon & Reindel, a prestigious top-40 law firm, Rodney instructed the driver to park on the sidewalk and wait for us, we would be back soon.

We walked into the building toward the elevators. A young man spotted Rodney and boarded the elevator with us. As we ascended, the kid pulled out the emergency stop button. I looked at him in disbelief and said, "What do you think you're doing?"

He responded, "I want to tell my friends that I was hanging out with Rodney."

Rodney interjected as he reached to adjust the tie he wasn't wearing, "You see, Bri, no respect. I get no respect."

Having told the building security personnel over the intercom that we were okay, I disengaged the "stop" button and we were on our way. The receptionist at the law offices guided us to the conference room where Rodney was to be deposed. Inside were two lawyers from Cahill Gordon & Reindel, a senior and a junior partner, the in-house general counsel from NBC, a woman of fifty-two to fifty-four years of age, and a female court reporter in her mid-thirties. As soon as Rodney walked in he said, "Hi, fellas, I'm here." When the NBC attorney didn't seem excited to see him, he said, "What's the matter with her?"

Having prepped Rodney for his deposition, as with all clients, he was instructed to simply answer the questions posed to him, with a "Yes" or "No," when possible, with no long-winded answers. No story telling.

The third generic question about Rodney's career elicited a response that lasted one and a half to two minutes. In plain view of my opposing counsel, I repeatedly punched Rodney in his left upper thigh region so that he would get the point that he was answering beyond the scope of the question. A few questions later Rodney asked for a bathroom break. As he limped away from the table, he turned to the two Cahill Gordon attorneys, looked at his thigh, and asked, "Do any of you guys know a good lawyer that I could hire to sue my lawyer?"

Controlling Dangerfield in a deposition was as easy as predicting the weather. He was pure Rodney, no different from his monologues at Dangerfield's. He was asked if he was ever deposed before and he said yeah once when he rented a house in Florida and the air conditioning broke down and he sweated like a pig. He asked if we could go off the record, and I instructed the court reporter to stop taking notes. Rodney turned to his new-found audience and said:

"So the lawyer during the deposition shows me my complaint and says, 'What do you mean by the claim that the owner of the home breached the implied covenant of habitability?' So I says to him, 'Can you speak English or what? Who taught you how to say those things?

What I'm telling you is I rented the house. I didn't rent a steam room or sauna. If I wanted to go to a spa, I would have. If I'm losing weight in the house without doing a thing, give me my money back.'"

Everybody laughed except NBC's counsel.

Two-thirds through the deposition, at Rodney's request, we went off the record again. Rodney turned to NBC's counsel and said, "Hey babe, I'll make you a deal. If you sleep with me, I'll drop the lawsuit." Everybody, including myself broke into hysterics. Ms. NBC was not amused. As soon as her hired guns saw the smoke emanating from her ears, they stopped their belly laughing, folded their hands, and looked contrite, like high-school students scolded by their teacher.

The NBC attorney looked at Rodney and authoritatively noted with conviction in a stern voice, "If you and I were the last two people on this planet, and we were on a deserted island, I would not sleep with you."

Rodney countered, "Hey, babe, that's your loss."

The deposition ended a few hours later, and sure enough the limo was parked halfway onto the sidewalk when we exited the building. As we drove back to my midtown law office, Rodney began to relax.

"Hey Bri, I'm glad that's over with." A second later he pulled out a crumbled napkin from his pocket, noting that he was a real "pothead" as he retrieved a joint. As if on cue, the driver rolled up the glass partition separating the front seat from the rear of the limo. As Rodney puffed away, he confirmed that he was "the comedian of the people. A jury is going to love me." Who was I to argue?

Rodney was just about done with the joint when we got to 42nd and Fifth Avenue. I could barely see the driver through the smoke screen in front of me. As I opened the door to leave, a cloud followed me out of the car like a scene from Cheech and Chong's *Up in Smoke*. Rodney came to attention and yelled, "Thanks Bri, you're all right."

25.
The Jerky Boys

Who knew that our childhood pranks could turn into a money-making proposition? The answer: two guys from Queens and a record label willing to take a chance on them. During the 1990s, Johnny Brennan and Kamal Ahmed revolutionized the way we considered and appreciated prank phone calls by creating innovative characters and plot settings to stage their theater of the absurd. In the process, they sold millions of comedy records and became a household name among the 14- to 22-year-old demographic. Sol Rosenberg, Frank Rizzo, the auto mechanic, the car salesman, Tarbash the Egyptian Magician, and Big Ole Badass Bob the Cattle Rustler were among their characters. Jerky Boy–isms caught on with phrases like:

Sizzle chest
Hey there tough guy
You're so silly
Rubber neck
Liver lips
Milky Licker
Piss Clams
Hey, Jerky

The catch phrases became accepted vernacular.

The first case I handled for the Jerky Boys involved a claim by Lou Gatanas, a former collaborator with the group, who claimed that he was wrongfully ejected from the team. Mr. Gatanas sought a court order compelling Johnny and Kamal to take him back so he could once more be a "Jerky Boy." For the same reason that courts do not order spouses or business partners to remain together because, among other things, it would require day-to-day supervision, a court will not order a band to stay together as an ensemble. If a partner is kicked out of a partnership, he or she is entitled to a distribution of partnership assets and an accounting. In the case of a band, partnership assets can include rights in the band's name and recordings, publishing, merchandising, and touring income streams created while the band member was part of the band.

As a predicate to denying Mr. Gatonas's application, our judge noted that in his thirty-five years on the bench he had never encountered anyone who wanted to be known as a "Jerky Boy."

Over the years I would handle a number of cases for Johnny and Kamal.

Prior to the release of *The Jerky Boys: The Movie* in 1995, I decided to treat Johnny and Kamal to a night out starting with a visit to the steam room and then massages at the 10th Street Russian & Turkish baths, followed by dinner at Smith & Wollensky's. When we were done with our steams and massages and on our way to grab some steak, Kamal asked me if I had been manhandled by my masseuse as he had been by his. Believing that he was pulling my leg, I asked him what he was talking about. Kamal emphatically noted that the young woman in the room had "smacked his pud around" and "yanked on it so hard that if she was Tarzan, she would have been swinging on it like a vine in Africa."

Not falling for the word of a Jerky Boy, I said that he was full of shit. Turns out he wasn't, as I later learned that the bathhouse was famous at that time for "happy endings."

Their inscribed photo in my office reads:

"Thank you so much for all your help in making my pockets much lighter. I can run so much faster now. You're such a silly bastard. Thank you." Signed by JB "Frank Rizzo" and Kamal.

26.
My Cousin Vinny

The year was 1998, six years after Joe Pesci and Marisa Tomei had starred in *My Cousin Vinny*. Pesci had secured a recording agreement with Sony Music, controlled by Tommy Mottola, and released his debut album of lounge music entitled *Vincent LaGuardia Gambini Sings for You*, featuring the wildly acclaimed single "Yo Cousin Vinny" that nobody ever heard of. Rumor had it that Pesci's family members bought seven copies of the album, which had accounted for 90 percent of the album sales to date.

When the call came in to represent Mr. Pesci in a music industry copyright infringement case, my first thought was, When did he become a recording artist? Often an entertainment litigator has no contact with his client and deals strictly with the talent's transactional/contract attorney and/or his manager. This was one of those cases. I never met or spoke with Joe, yet he was my client and it was my obligation to represent him zealously whether I met him or not.

Joe and his coauthor were accused of plagiarism, a claim they vehemently denied. The accuser was a publishing company that owned and administered an Italian tune, that was a favorite from a bygone era, entitled "Pepino, the Italian Mouse," released in 1962 by Lou Monte.

I was told that Pesci's coauthor, an elderly Italian gentleman named Don Roberto, would be made available for a debriefing so that I could mount a defense to the claim before us.

The attorney-client privilege is a doctrine that shields third-party intrusion, investigation, or discovery into the confidential communications between a lawyer and client relating to legal advice, as long as no unrelated third-party is present.

Joe, at the time, was represented by an old-timer named Jay Julien, and it was at his offices that I was to meet Don Roberto. When I arrived, I was shown into an interior small conference room where a little old man was sitting at a round table, and two larger Italian-looking gentlemen in identical turtlenecks and blazers were leaning against and "holding up" the walls.

My first instinct was to ask the two dapper dons to identify themselves so that I could excuse them from the room to avoid losing the "privilege" with any communications I had with Don Roberto. Then it dawned on me that maybe the movie references to Pesci being a "made man" were not fictional and I would be taking my life into my own hands by demanding that these fine upstanding citizens identify themselves, then leave the room.

After conducting a forty-five-second balancing act in my brain, I concluded that I could get some general background information from Don Roberto without imparting any legal advice until I ascertained who the two dudes were. Don Roberto recounted in detail how the song was created as I took notes. To my surprise, each of the two wall-flowers understood musical concepts and were peppering Don Roberto with questions and ideas to help refresh his recollection. I was at a total loss to understand how these fine gentlemen were knowledgeable about melody, harmony, note progression, tempo, and instrumentation. Finally, my curiosity could be suppressed no more. "Who are you guys?"

"I'm Tommy DeVito of the Four Seasons, and this is Al Nittoli." Nittoli, an actor who had worked with Pesci on *Casino*, was also known as his "stand-in." No wonder I thought the guys against the wall might be connected.

As a result of the information I learned at my meeting, I was able to interpose a viable defense to the claim of copyright infringement. After months of negotiations, the case ultimately settled for a song and a dance.

27

"YMCA":
An Iconic American Song

In Brooklyn, during 1977 and 1978, my Italian and Jewish buddies and I would go cruising in my mother's 1974 Plymouth Gold Duster, a totally "uncool" car. *Saturday Night Fever* had been released and disco had taken over. Everybody wanted to be Tony Minero (the John Travolta character). Wearing colorful polyester shirts with three top buttons opened, hairy chests exposed with a gold Italian devil's horn or a pair of dice dangling, we were ready for action. Driving around Bensonhurst and Sheepshead Bay, my high-school mates and I were well prepared for any confrontation that might await us with other "tough guys." A crow bar was neatly nestled to my left and a Yankee's slugger baseball bat made of ash was snuggled between the driver and passenger seat. My radio was usually turned up blasting songs by the Bee Gees, the Village People, and K.C. and the Sunshine Band. Our favorite tune of the time was "Macho Man." When it played, if we were stopped at a red light, we would get out and dance around the car until irate drivers behind us honked their horns at us in disgust.

Victor Willis, the original lead singer and lyricist of the Village People, coauthored "YMCA," "Macho Man," and "In the Navy," among other Village People releases. Like many young recording artists and songwriters, he signed a one-sided and somewhat oppressive agreement relating to his recording and songwriting services back in the 1970s. With respect to his work as a songwriter, he agreed to accept royalty participations of anywhere from 18 to 22 percent, even though he wrote all the lyrics or half of the songs he was involved in.

In 1976, Congress enacted new legislation overhauling the

United States Copyright Act of 1909. One of the new provisions of the Act allowed creators and artists in all genres—music, literature, art, and motion pictures among others—the right to terminate grants or assignments of copyright for works created after 1978, thirty-five years after their creation. The statutory scheme required a majority of the grantors on a particular grant to give a minimum of two years advance notice to terminate their grant and reacquire their copyright interests in the United States, during a five-year window to do so, subject to a few qualifications. The purpose behind the statute was to redress the unequal bargaining power between artists of all walks of life and the entities with whom they did business early in their careers, when nobody knew the true value their creations would one day have. "Workers for hire," those individuals akin to employees, did not have this right of termination, but all other creators did.

In 2011, Willis, through his attorneys, sent notice to Willis's music publisher to terminate his copyright grants from 1978 and 1979 relating to twenty-four musical compositions he coauthored, including "YMCA." His publisher, Can't Stop the Music, took the position that Willis was one of three authors on the songs and did not have "standing" to terminate his grants. In a case of first impression interpreting the copyright termination statutory provisions, the Federal District Court for the Southern District of California in San Diego found that since Willis executed his publishing agreements alone, he was the sole grantor on his grants and thus had standing to terminate them. Willis learned for the first time in August 2009 that Henri Belolo, a Frenchman, whose partner in business, Jacques Morali, conceived of and was instrumental in forming the Village People band, was claiming to have authored in French the lyrics to all the subject Village People songs prior to Willis having created his lyrics to each.

Belolo claimed that Willis, who did not speak, read, or write French, had somehow "adapted" or translated Belolo's French lyrics into English. While none of the claimed twenty-four French songs was ever commercially released in France, French sheet music for each composition was prepared and released for sale in France in the months following the commercial release in the United States of each of the corresponding twenty-four recordings in English. Belolo had no evidence of having written any songs in French, either in the form of handwritten notes or typed lyric sheets. In addition, the alleged French lyrics were never synched with the music that was ultimately used in the commercial releases of the songs in the US. A number of other songwriters, who had signed "adaptation agreements" with Can't Stop The Music, came forward and said that no prior French lyrics existed when they wrote English lyrics for various songs from scratch, and that Belolo also claimed coauthorship credit on their songs even though he had not participated in the songwriting process.

In February 2015, we were scheduled to go to trial. The only issues to be tried before the jury were whether Belolo was a coauthor on each of the twenty-four songs, i.e., did he write them in French before Willis wrote them in English, with Willis having used the French versions in the process, and whether Willis had waited too long to assert his claim. If Willis brought his claim in a timely fashion and was deemed to be the sole lyricist, he would be entitled to fifty percent interest on each of the twenty-four songs, instead of the one-third interest that the court had already awarded him.

The jury heard our case over two weeks. The Village People Indian even made a guest appearance following the judge's admonition that he not show up in costume. There were repeated fireworks from the outset. Nothing went unchallenged or without a contentious confrontation. Even the jury selection process had its moments, starting with my objection to the challenge to strike from the jury a black high-school principal and former band member by Belolo's lawyer. At my client's urging, I claimed that the challenge was racially motivated and biased. However, since there was only one African American among our entire empaneled jury pool of thirty-five members, the judge correctly reasoned that he could see no pattern to justify my protestations.

My opening statement painted Monsieur Belolo as a sophisticated businessman who had perpetrated a massive scheme over thirty-five years by falsely listing himself as a coauthor on twenty-four songs he did not write.

When it came to the pivotal song "YMCA," Willis testified about growing up in Oakland, California, and routinely going to a YMCA there to participate in sports and meet people. When he moved to New York as a young man trying to break into the theater and music industry, he frequented another YMCA on the Upper West Side of Manhattan. Willis told about and identified the inspirations that lead him to write the lyrics to "YMCA."

Henri Belolo, on the other hand, admitted to the jury on my cross-examination that in his entire life he had never been inside a YMCA. He claimed that he wrote French lyrics to a song called "La Vie de Bon Coté" (translated to "Life on the Good Side"), *before* he had ever thought of doing a song about a YMCA, and that Willis adapted that song from French to English. When asked then how could it be that the opening verse of "La Vie de bon Coté" started with the phrase "Jeune homme" ("young man") as did "YMCA," he stated it was simply a coincidence.

Belolo testified that he was proficient in English, even though French was his native language, and that he had translated English to French and French to English going back to the 1960s. He had no plausible explanation as to why he would write songs in French earmarked for the Village People to sing in English, when he could have written the songs in English in the first instance.

Belolo testified that even though the words and the music to "La Vie de Bon Coté" had been completed before the idea for "YMCA" had ever arisen, Belolo's own witness acknowledged that he had heard Belolo and Morali working on "La Vie de Bon Coté" while discussing "YMCA."

Belolo admitted that he did not collaborate with Willis on any of the songs at issue. Willis confirmed this fact and testified that he was not given and did not hear any French songs before he and he alone wrote the lyrics to "YMCA" and twenty-three other songs.

Closing arguments (summations) took over eight hours. The jury then deliberated for almost five full days before they reached a verdict. At the end, the jury determined that Willis's claims were not barred by the statute of limitations, and Belolo did not coauthor the lyrics to "YMCA" and twelve other songs despite his name having been on the copyright registrations to these works from 1979 to the time of the trial. Willis now was the rightful fifty percent owner of "YMCA" as the sole lyricist to that iconic song.

28.
Statutory Rape:
A Top 40 Shakedown

Statutory rape is a strict liability criminal offense, which means that if you have sexual intercourse with someone who is under the age allowed by state law to give consent for sex, you are criminally liable for statutory rape even if you thought your partner was of age. It is the public policy of each state to set an age of consent consistent with the social values of that jurisdiction. Accordingly, laws for statutory rape differ state by state with respect to the age to give consent.

My top 40 recording artist client had sexual relations with a young lady with a fake ID. No complaint was made to the local authorities and no criminal proceedings were commenced. Instead, six months after the event, enterprising attorneys sent my client a demand letter (in the name of the parents of the young lady, but on her behalf) accompanied by a draft complaint relating to the incident. The complaint alleged that the client had committed a civil assault (unpermitted bodily contact) and battery upon the claimant and sought millions of dollars in damages. While the attorneys for the claimant did not threaten to go to the district attorney's office with criminal charges, they knew that any public filing of the civil complaint would lead to widespread publicity and could lead to a criminal investigation.

Legal research revealed that there was a distinction between the age of consent for statutory rape purposes and whether a person below that age of consent could give consent to sexual relations as a complete defense to civil assault and battery claims. It turned out that no action for civil assault and battery was recognized in the two states at issue if the sexual conduct was not forced upon or against the will of the claimant. While this legal principle should have eviscerated the claim-ant's claim, her attorneys rather unscrupulously said they were prepared to file the complaint unless a settlement was reached. Unwilling to run the risk of a public filing of a civil complaint leading to a criminal inves-tigation against my client, he acquiesced to the legal blackmail and paid a significant sum to settle the claim, with both a structured settlement over time and a confidentiality clause with a forfeiture provision attached to it. The complaint never saw the light of day.

29.
I Coulda Been a Contender:
Million Dollar Quartet

State law determines whether an individual's right of privacy and publicity, prohibiting third-party use of an individual's name and likeness for commercial purposes, descends to an individual's estate after their death. California and Tennessee have enacted legislation giving estates descendible rights of privacy and publicity. New York has no such laws. The residency of the entertainer at the time of death determines which state's law applies. For those states that do not recognize rights of privacy and publicity for deceased individuals, the estates of such parties have no legal authority to control name and likeness rights.

The call of a lifetime came in to me in 2010. I was asked to represent the estates of Elvis Presley, Johnny Cash, and Carl Perkins in connection with the alleged unauthorized use of their names and likenesses by a Broadway production company that was putting on a show called "Million Dollar Quartet." The show chronicled a jam session that took place on December 4, 1956, between Presley, Cash, Perkins, and Jerry Lee Lewis. Mr. Lewis was still alive and would be represented by other counsel. To say I was honored to represent these three iconic estates would be an understatement. After careful consideration, I drafted a demand letter to the producers of the show laying out our position. Attorney representatives for each of the three estates reviewed and approved the letter before it was sent. Upon receipt of my letter, negotiations commenced between the parties and within a week the claim was resolved.

My extremely high-profile lawsuit would never be filed.

30.
Who Knew the Stripper Could Sing?

For a number of years, I represented a Westchester County–based company that furnished bands for weddings, bar mitzvahs, and other parties. They had a stable of over twelve bands, and interested clients would frequently see and hear at least two or three bands perform before they made their selection. One of the more accomplished bands, often in high demand, featured a seven-person ensemble including a strikingly attractive and dynamic lead singer who could give Ella Fitzgerald a run for her money. The band was booked regularly on Saturdays and Sundays and had an avid following.

As it turns out, the lead singer of the band moonlighted as a stripper for bachelor parties to make some extra money. So too, the best laid plans of mice and men often go awry. In this case the singer of the band was hired by the best man of the groom to perform as the main attraction at a Friday night bachelor party. Everybody had a good time.

Two days later, as luck would have it, the singer was performing again, but this time fully clothed in front of the groom, his bride, and approximately a hundred and ninety invited guests. By the time it took the attendees of the bachelor party to realize the stripper was now in a new get-up and singing, she had only sung a handful of notes. Before long, word of mouth spread like wild fire and the bride was told that the magnificent singer had other talents. The resulting displeasure led to a lawsuit against the band-furnishing company. Unfortunately, the most important day in this young woman's (the bride's) life ended on a sour note.

The claims against my client included breach of contract and the negligent infliction of emotional distress. The bachelor party attendees simply thought the singer was overdressed for the occasion.

31.
The Ugly Duckling

On a cold winter day, the well-respected but extremely homely comedian came to our office with a significant problem. A woman with whom he had had an evening of carnal knowledge claimed to be the mother of his child. Her choice of a suitor left a lot to be desired. Our client, A. J., had a face that only a mother could have liked and a voice that would lead you to buy sound-eliminating headphones.

Rather than go public with her accusation, our client's alleged paramour had engaged a noted high-profile attorney who specialized in divorce, paternity, and palimony proceedings. The demand letter claiming that our funny man was now a not-so-funny father was received certified mail return receipt requested in an envelope marked "personal and confidential." There was more bargaining power to be had by keeping our client's indiscretion private with the threat of going public if we did not work things out.

Under New York law at the time, child support obligations in a court-contested paternity proceeding could result in a payment obligation, equaling as much as twenty-five percent of a noncustodial parent's income.

A. J., with his one-liners, paced the hallway of our law office dazed, confused, and muttering:

"How can this be?"

"No this can't be?"

"It wasn't me!"

"Somebody else is responsible!"

"What can we do here?"

"Oy vey! How did I get myself into this predicament?"

"This isn't even funny."

We sat A. J. down and explained to him that he would have no obligations whatsoever unless paternity was definitively proven and that prevailing HLA testing had a 98- to 99-percent accuracy rate in establishing paternity. The thought of being a father again late in his life did not appeal to A. J., who was well past his prime.

Over the course of a few weeks, discussions were had with opposing counsel as to how to proceed. We requested an HLA test of the baby and the other side requested the same from our would-be "dad." Before we agreed to any particular protocol, it was suggested that our respective clients with their attorneys have a face-to-face meeting at our office.

The day of reckoning was upon us. A. J. arrived thirty minutes early in a heavy winter coat and did his best to wear out a track in our carpet. As if an expectant father outside the delivery room at the hospital, he paced back and forth. When I saw the very attractive young lady arrive at the elevator bank with a baby stroller in tow, I couldn't help but think that most men would have been proud to have sired her child. But A. J. was clearly thirty to thirty-five years her senior, so what was she thinking? I guess women go for a good sense of humor.

I imagined some of the one liners A. J would have told her in bed:

"It's really bigger than it looks."

"It goes into shrivel mode to camouflage itself."

"If only I was thirty again, this would be easier."

"Don't laugh until we are done."

Our adversary arrived a few minutes later and it was now time to get to work.

We all gathered in a conference room for the "meet and confer" that was about to take place. A. J. was uneasy and wanted to be somewhere else. After some pleasantries were exchanged and it was confirmed that all communications that day were off the record and for settlement purposes only, the mother approached her child. The baby was gingerly lifted from the stroller and the blanket and protective coverings that shielded him from the cold were removed. All eyes were on the newborn. A silence came over the room. Three attorneys who normally liked to hear their own voices fell mute. Everyone stared at the baby. He could have been the ugliest baby that I had ever seen. Even A. J. could not believe his eyes. In the baby he saw a "Mini-Me" before there even was a such a thing as a "Mini-Me." A. J.'s jaw dropped. We all agreed to take a short break for each side to caucus.

Fifteen minutes later we came back to the conference room. We confirmed that no blood tests would be necessary and that A. J. would acknowledge paternity.

The apple did not fall far from the tree.

32.
"Only Little People Pay Taxes"—
Leona and Harry Helmsley

What you say can come back and bite you.

The year was 1986, and I had been a lawyer for less than a year. Harry Helmsley, the billionaire real estate developer in New York City, who had at one point in time been a leading Quaker, had recently engaged our firm. In 1972, Harry had married Leona Roberts, a successful real estate broker who had swept him off his feet. Their real estate empire included the Helmsley Palace Hotel, the Park Lane Hotel, the St. Moritz, the Helmsley Building (also known as the Lincoln Building), and many other holdings. Through a number of partnerships and other legal entities, the Helmsleys also had ownership interests in the Empire State Building and the Flatiron Building. Harry and Leona lived in a 23,000-square-foot, twenty-eight room mansion known as Dunnellen Hall in Greenwich, Connecticut, and had a huge apartment in Manhattan with a full-length indoor swimming pool located at the Park Lane. As Harry had gotten on in age, he slowly but surely ceded control of his vast holdings to Leona, who ruled their dynasty with an iron fist. To say that Leona alienated a few people in her lifetime would be an understatement. She mistreated and fired people on a regular basis and was given the moniker the "Queen of Mean."

In 1986, Parcher Arisohn & Hayes was engaged by Harry and Leona to handle a number of personal cases for them as well as cases for their hotels and Helmsley Spears. One of the cases was brought by Remco Maintenance Co., against Harry and Leona personally for marble maintenance work done at Dunnellen Hall. Remco invoices totaling hundreds of thousands of dollars had not been paid and I was assigned the task of going to Dunnellen Hall to assess the quality of the condition of the marble located throughout the property.

The defense that had been interposed to the complaint was that the work performed for the Helmsleys had been done in an inferior and unprofessional way, a common theme among Leona's disdain to pay for services rendered. Whether or not she had a paranoia that all contractors sought to gouge her and Harry, she put each of them through trials and tribulations before they were paid a discount off their original bills with no interest for the delay in payment.

I drove from White Plains to Greenwich and found the elite Round Hill Road where Dunnellen Hall was located. When I got to the security gate of the "Hall" a rather large guard with an attack dog approached my vehicle to sniff me out. In my suit and tie I apparently did not pose a threat, and after announcing that I was one of the Helmsleys' lawyers, I was directed where and how to proceed. No Helmsley rep was there to greet me or show me around. I had all the open invoices with me and began comparing the charges with the locations where the work was done. I started with the swimming pool area and the marble Greek and Roman sculptures that were strewn around it. Next, I tackled the seventeenth-century Italian marble gazebo. I was welcomed into the home by one of the housekeepers and announced who I was. Inside, I surveyed the marble floors in a handful of larger meeting/public rooms. Finally, I went through the fourteen bedrooms to survey the nine marble fireplaces. The staff went about their business, and I was given free rein to walk about the monstrosity. In the living room I found antiques, a number of them haphazardly placed around the room as if they were new acquisitions. A beautiful green malachite table had its 64,000 dollar price sticker still hanging down from a leg.

When I got to what appeared to be the master bedroom by

reason of its size differential, I sat on the edge of the bed facing the fireplace taking notes. After a minute or two a woman staff member peeked in and saw me. In a terribly agitated way she said, "Quick, quick, get up! If she sees you, we'll all be fired." I rose from the bed in disbelief and made sure to complete my analysis standing. When I finished my inspection of the last fireplace I was done. The irony of the day was that since I had not seen any of the marble items before Remco's work, I had no baseline to compare the finished items to.

On the eve of Leona's deposition, the case settled.

In 1988, someone dropped a dime on the Helmsleys with the *New York Post*, and the reporter doing the exposé called Howard Rubinstein, the publicist for the Helmsleys, and gave him three days to respond to the allegations he had been given. Some of the claims related to the billing of personal expenses by the Helmsleys to Helmsley-owned business entities.

Leona had an assistant/hatchet man named Frank Turco who, like many others, had been unceremoniously fired when he displeased Leona. I was directed to go to the offices of Helmsley-Spear and review Turco's files. I was put in a room with three long banker boxes full of documents and began reviewing what was before me. As if assembling a road map for a conviction, the files I reviewed contained a plethora of documentation that ultimately became the basis for Leona and Harry's indictments for tax evasion, creating false business records, and other sundry charges. There were original invoices from numerous vendors addressed to Mr. & Mrs. Harry Helmsley at Dunnellen Hall followed by anywhere from one to four invoices from the same vendors for the same work with typed-in addresses for Helmsley-owned businesses. The phony back-up invoices each bore payment initials of Harry and Leona.

Leona was convicted in 1989 on charges of federal tax evasion. Although Harry had been indicted with Leona in 1988, he was deemed too weak mentally to assist his attorneys in his own defense. When Leona's son passed, she refused to pay for his funeral. When Leona passed, she left millions to her dog. Try to figure people out. You can't.

33.
Lou Reed and the Espresso Machine

Lou Reed and John Cale, members of The Velvet Underground, were both musical and cultural icons, and I was honored to be retained to represent them in a case against Universal Music. Lou and John could not have had more different personalities. Lou was prickly, distant, and impatient, with a chip on his shoulder. John was friendly, outgoing, and personable.

I defended each in depositions against a very capable opposing counsel. John's deposition went smoothly. Lou, somewhat understandably, would have rather been somewhere else. Although I was Lou's protector during the process, he was a bit disdainful toward me. He acted as if I was his dentist getting ready to pull teeth. During a short recess during the deposition, Lou asked if he could get "a good cup of coffee." The next thing I knew Lou and opposing counsel were talking about espresso machines and varieties of coffee, subjects that were unfamiliar to me. Feeling left out I realized there was no way I could interrupt and talk about the New York Yankees, Abraham Lincoln and the Civil War, or fishing, subjects in which I was well versed.

Before long, Lou and the other attorney were going back to his office so that Lou could savor one of my adversary's fresh-made cappuccinos. I sat in the large conference room with the court reporter thinking to myself that Lou was getting along better with my adversary than he was with me. What a crazy world. About ten minutes later Lou came back with cappuccino in hand. My opposing counsel had a grin on his face when he said that he "didn't froth milk for just anybody." The deposition concluded without incident. Lou and John's case against Universal ultimately settled after I met with Lou at a café and discussed the settlement points over a good cup of cappuccino. At no time did I ever froth Lou's milk.

34.
Buddhism and Baseball

I was attending a lavish dinner party in Delhi, India, in April of 2017. Among the dignitaries and politicians present were billionaires, members of India's parliament, journalists, authors, bankers, and other assorted movers and shakers. My good friends, Jay and Jagi Panda, were hosting the gathering in their home on a hot and humid evening typical of the central India climate that time of year. Two partners from my law firm and I were doing our best to mingle and work the room, making new contacts when we could. Jay was incredibly gracious and did everything possible to facilitate our introduction to the cream of society. My partners and I were energetic although somewhat fatigued from a nine-hour car ride back from the Jim Corbett Tiger Reserve in Uttar Pradesh earlier in the day.

As I was saying "nice to meet you" to my seventeenth guest, Jay tapped me on the shoulder. "Brian, I would like to introduce you to someone special." I turned around. "This is Lobsang Sangay, the prime minister in exile from Tibet." As I reached to extend my hand, Jay continued, "Sangay, this is Brian, a good friend of mine and a lawyer from New York whom I've known for over thirty years."

The prime minister had begun to reach his hand out to mine when he heard Jay utter the words that I was from New York. Sangay immediately withdrew his hand, squinted his eyes as if he were about to start a cross-examination and in a serious tone with a bit of possible contempt looked me straight in the eyes and said, "Are you a Yankees fan?"

I had not completed getting the words out of my mouth— "I am a diehard Yankees fan"—and Sangay was off to the races.

"The Red Sox are god's gift to baseball!"

"The Yankees have been, will be, and are the enemy!"

"When it comes to Red Sox-Yankees baseball you can throw Buddhism right out the window and the Dalai Lama has no intervention rights."

Hoping to ask Sangay some more profound questions, I waited for him to pause and thought of the appropriate queries for him: "What's it like to be in exile?" "How do you deal with China's opposition to the very existence of Tibet and its marginalization of your people?" "When the Dalai Lama passes, how will that affect your day-to-day existence?"

Unfortunately Sangay's pro-Red Sox/anti-Yankees rant continued on and on for what seemed like an eternity. I thought that if Sangay had half as much passion for Tibet as he did for the Red Sox, Tibet would be well served.

When Sangay finally stopped for air, I sensed I had an opening. I'd gone to many Yankee games each year. "I would be honored to take you to a Yankees/Red Sox game if you come to New York." Sangay again got serious, looked me in the eyes as he folded his arms and said, "I will only go with you to a Red Sox/Yankees game if the Red Sox are going to win."

I would later learn that Lobsang Sangay, whose name means the "Kind-hearted Lion," was only forty-nine years old, had been born to Tibetan refugees living in Darjeeling in Northern India, and had lived a challenging life, achieving in the face of adversity. Following rigorous training in a Tibetan school in Darjeeling, Sangay received B.A. and LL.B degrees from the University of Delhi in India, and was then offered a Fulbright Scholarship to Harvard Law School. It was in Cambridge, Massachusetts, that Sangay became a Red Sox fan.

On April 27, 2011, Sangay was elected Kalön Tripa of the Tibetan Government-in-Exile with 55 percent of the votes. As prime minister, he has emphasized the importance of seeking a peaceful, nonviolent solution to the Tibet issue.

But sometimes baseball is more important than world politics or the meaning of life taught to us by profound religions.

35.
Whitey Ford—
The Chairman of the Board

It has not been too often that after the age of forty I acted like I was twelve again. The year was 2003, and I was in the office of Bert Padell, a well-known CPA and business manager who, over the years, had represented many stars. Bert lived a charmed life. He was the batboy for the Yankees in 1949 and 1950, when he was sixteen and seventeen. He met and intermingled with Joe DiMaggio, Yogi Berra, Mickey Mantle, and Whitey Ford. The Yankees won the World Series each year he was there. Bert ultimately became an accountant and built up an impressive practice. Over the years he represented a cadre of actors, music performers, and athletes, a who's who of celebrities from the 1960s through 2010. Over the years, Bert's clients had included DiMaggio, Mantle, Russell Simmons, Biggie Smalls, Madonna, Alicia Keys, Britney Spears, and others. Bert was a warm, energetic, and engaging man.

This particular day, I was scheduled to meet Bert to discuss a matter involving Britney Spears. Bert's office was a collector's paradise of memorabilia. Between gold and platinum records, signed presidential, music, and sports memorabilia, and three-dimensional amusements of all kinds, Bert's place was a visual wonderland. Upon my arrival, I was told by the receptionist that it would be a few minutes before I could see Bert as he was in with Whitey Ford. As a lifelong Yankees fan, my jaw dropped. After quickly regrouping, I inquired as to whether it was possible to meet Mr. Ford prior to his departure. One call to Bert later and I was told to go in. Bert introduced me as a litigator who did work for his clients. As I shook Whitey's hand,

Bert asked Whitey if he wanted to join us for lunch. When he said, "Sure," I couldn't believe it.

If I could have hired a videographer to film our lunch I would have. Hanging out with the "Chairman of the Board," a Yankees icon with a lifetime record of 236-106 and a 2.75 ERA, and winner of ten World Series games, was a dream come true. Whitey was drinking white wine spritzers and regaling us with stories. He was charming. Billy Martin, Joe DiMaggio, Yogi Berra, and Mickey Mantle—he told anecdotes about each one. I ate it up like a seven-year-old devours an ice cream cone with sprinkles.

Whitey was opening a new restaurant on Long Island and was interested in borrowing one piece of memorabilia from Bert, a 1950 World Series bat used and inscribed by Joe DiMaggio. When Bert had been the Yankees batboy in 1950, so the story goes, he was given seven new five-dollar bills by DiMaggio as a tip. He frowned. DiMaggio said, "What's the matter kid, isn't that enough?" Bert responded, "I really would like the bat you used today." DiMaggio took the thirty-five dollars back and gave Bert a stamped World Series 1950 baseball bat autographed and inscribed by Joe, "To Bert Padell, continued success to you—a Yankee teammate. Joe DiMaggio."

Bert played hardball with Whitey and wouldn't relent when it came to loaning the bat. "You can borrow anything else you want," he said. Our meal flew by, but the memories were to last a lifetime.

A few years later, through Bert, I was actually engaged to represent Whitey in an action where his name and likeness had been used without his permission. He was a gentleman throughout my representation of him.

36.
Ralph Branca—
The Shot Heard Around the World

Ralph Branca, the former Brooklyn Dodger was referred to me by Bert Padell. Ralph was charismatic, entertaining, and affable. The third line into our meeting he said, "You know they stole the sign for the pitch." Ralph, a three-time All Star with the Dodgers was best known for his short relief appearance in the 1951 National League playoff game at the Polo Grounds against the New York Giants, the Dodger's crosstown rivals.

Branca entered the game in the ninth inning with one out and runners on second and third, facing the Giants outfielder Bobby Thomson. Bobby hit "The Shot Heard 'Round the World," a home run to left field that propelled the Giants to win the pennant. It was a devastating loss for Ralph and the Dodgers.

Of greater significance, yet less well-known, is the fact that Ralph was a member of the Dodgers in April 1947 when Jackie Robinson broke the color barrier and became the first African American ballplayer to play in the major leagues. Ralph, at six foot four, stood next to Jackie, who was five foot nine, on the first base line at Ebbets Field when the National Anthem was played to start the game. According to Ralph, later that day his brother called him and screamed at him for standing next to Jackie as there had been threats that a sharpshooter might look to take Jackie out, and if he missed, Ralph might've been hit.

Branca gave me a signed baseball for my collection which reads: "April 15, 1947, Ebbets Field, New York, Me and Jackie Robinson standing on the first base line. You should have been there." Signed, Ralph Branca.

I successfully represented Ralph in a case against a baseball memorabilia maven.

37.
Mike Tyson—
The Young Champ with a
Sparkle in His Eye

The year was 1988. Mike Tyson was the heavyweight champion of the world. He had knocked out Trevor Berbick in the second round, winning the WBC heavyweight title in November 1986, to become the youngest heavyweight champion in history at age twenty. In March 1987, Tyson had defeated James "Bonecrusher" Smith to win the WBA heavyweight title. And in August 1987, he overpowered Tony Tucker to capture the IBF championship, unifying the heavyweight title. By 1988, Tyson was comanaged by Jimmy Jacobs and Bill Cayton. Following Jacobs's death in March, Tyson retained Parcher Arisohn & Hayes to assess his rights. We were ultimately engaged to seek a judicial decree that Tyson had legally appropriate grounds to terminate his contractual and managerial relationship with Bill Cayton.

The first time "Iron Mike" came to our offices at 500 Fifth Avenue, Peter Parcher, our dynamic and theatrical head partner, introduced Mike to me in our main conference room noting that I was an associate attorney at the firm, had worked ninety hours on Mike's case over the last week, and said I wanted to fight Mike when the case was over. With a twinkle in his eye and a Cheshire cat grin, Tyson leaned across the conference room table, extended his bulky limb and shook my hand with a vicelike grip, emphasis added. My hand, which had been engulfed and consumed by his, quietly exited looking a bit like overcooked spaghetti in a heap. Following Tyson's departure from our offices, I ran into mine with my mangled right paw. I called my best friend, dialing the number with my left hand while my right one pulsated.

With jubilance, I explained, "I just met Iron Mike, but I think he broke my hand."

It would only be a short time later that Tyson would knock out a previously undefeated Michael Spinks in 91 seconds on June 27, 1988, at the Trump Plaza Hotel and Casino in Atlantic City. The fight, the richest in boxing history to that point, grossed more than seventy million dollars with Tyson earning more than twenty million dollars.

Some judges like the spotlight, some do not. In the case of *Tyson v. Cayton*, Justice Bruce Wright of the Supreme Court of the State of New York, did not enjoy the fanfare or publicity associated with the case assigned to him. He wished to broker a settlement between the parties, if at all possible, and remove the case from his docket. During one particular court date in July 1988, Justice Wright requested the Tyson side meet in his chambers while the Cayton side met in a nearby jury room. We sat around a large circular wood table: Tyson, Donald Trump (one of Tyson's so-called "advisors"), Peter Parcher, Steve Hayes, me, and Michael Winston, a lawyer advisor to Mike procured by his mother-in-law Ruth Roper (Robin Givens's mother). Trump and his ego took up most of the room. Tyson, who had defeated Spinks only a few weeks earlier, was being cajoled by Trump to talk about the fight. Soft-spoken Mike, talking slightly louder than a whisper, said he could see the fear in Spinks's eyes when the bell for the first round rang and he entered the ring. He "knew he had him." Tyson pursued him like a predator pursues its wounded prey and delivered the knock-out blow in record time. What had been billed as the largest grossing fight of all time ended almost before it began. Tyson was fearless and fearsome.

Trump took over the conversation again and started talking about George Foreman's boxing comeback story. In 1987, Foreman, after ten years in retirement, surprised the boxing world by announcing a comeback at the age of thirty-eight. He publicly stated that he wished to fight Tyson. Foreman had won five fights in '87 and a handful more in '88 as he slimmed down and returned to fighting form, although much slower than in his youth.

Trump, always the instigator, turned to Mike and asked about Foreman's string of successes on the comeback trail. Tyson noted that George was an old man now and the opponents he fought were "scrubs." Trump asked if Mike would consider fighting George. Tyson said, "I can't fight the man. I'd kill him." Trump began his badgering: "If a pot of money was put in front of you, would you fight Foreman?" Tyson retorted: "I don't want to kill the man." Trump, conducting his own personal cross-examination, came back at him again. "That wasn't my question. The only thing I want to know is for the right amount of money would you fight him." Tyson hesitated and thought for a moment, smiled, his gold front tooth shimmering in the light, and sheepishly said, "For the right amount of money, I'd do anything."

38.
Jugoplastika v. The Boston Celtics—
"Poaching From a Stocked Pond"

Dino Radja, a six foot ten power forward, was a star player for the Jugoplastika basketball team of Split, Yugoslavia (now Croatia). He was on the Yugoslavia Olympic basketball team that won the silver medal in the 1988 Olympic Games in Seoul, South Korea. Together with Toni Kukoc they propelled Jugoplastika to the European Cup Championships in 1989. Like most Eastern Europeans living under totalitarian regimes, Radja, even though a national and local star, dreamed of greener pastures and financial success. Many of the luxuries of Western life were not available in Split or Belgrade, the capital of Yugoslavia, each of which was under the dominion of a socialist federation government founded by Marshal Tito in 1943 and still in effect in 1989, ten years after his death. Jugoplastika, although not a professional team by American standards, had written employment agreements with its players, many of whom had been groomed by the team since their youth. Team players had numerous amenities and privileges that were not available to the average Yugoslavian citizen, but they would never get rich playing basketball in their country.

In June 1989, Radja, then twenty-two, who was earning eleven thousand dollars per year with Jugoplastika, got drafted by the Boston Celtics. That same summer, Vlade Divac, Drozen Petrovic, and Zerko Pespalj, three fellow Yugoslavs, were joining the NBA. Radja was still under contract with the Jugoplastika team and its general manager, Josip Bilic, insisted that Radja honor his contract through 1992. During August 1989, Radja travelled to the United States and in defiance of his obligations to Jugoplastika signed a one-year deal with the

Celtics, who paid him 425,000 dollars. Radja began publicly working out with the team at my alma mater, Brandeis University in Waltham, Massachusetts. Shortly thereafter, officials from team Jugoplastika reached out and retained Parcher Arisohn & Hayes.

Steve Hayes and I were tasked with flying to Yugoslavia to meet with team representatives to draft affidavits in support of an application to get an injunction against Radja and the Celtics, to prohibit Radja from playing basketball with the Celtics.

Steve and I flew to Belgrade, switched planes and landed in Split a few hours later. My luggage made a wrong turn and was missing in action. We were met at the airport by Bladen, one of the team representatives who could actually speak English, and another gentleman who didn't talk much. Bladen was extremely happy to meet the American lawyers who were going to help preserve a national resource and local asset. When he learned that I was without additional clothing, he said he would get me team apparel and not to worry. During our drive from the airport to the Jugoplastika facility we were pulled over by local police for speeding. When Bladen identified who Steve and I were the officers gave us a motorcade escort with sirens.

During our three days in Split, we worked around the clock using an interpreter to translate both documents and conversations with team officials. I was outfitted with oversized team shorts and a basketball shirt that loosely fit on my body until my suitcase finally arrived. We were proudly introduced to the team players who understood our mission was to get Radja back for the good of the team. Photos were taken with the team's seven foot tall center, a young man named Toni Kukoc, who ultimately played for the Chicago Bulls alongside Michael Jordan. Kukoc towered over us but was a good sport in our minimal interactions.

Steve and I worked hard, drafting and editing the affidavits that would ultimately be submitted in court in Boston to stop the Celtics from usurping Jugoplastika's star player. Throughout our stay we were treated like saviors and dignitaries. When we left Split our mandate was simple: bring Dino Radja home.

Our lawsuit was filed in the United States District Court for the District of Massachusetts seeking an injunction against Radja and the Celtics.

The Celtics took the position that Radja's contract with Jugoplastika was as an "amateur," akin to a college basketball player's commitment to play for a university, and not binding if the player decided to turn professional.

After a hearing on September 26, 1989, Judge Douglas Woodlock, comparing the Celtics's conduct to "poaching from a stocked pond," ruled against the Celtics and issued a preliminary injunction preventing Radja from playing for them during the remaining portion of his term of contract with Jugoplastika. We had prevailed!

Following the successful court ruling in favor of Jugoplastika, which effectively changed the balance of power between the mighty Celtics and Jugoplastika, the team nobody ever heard of in the United States (except a few basketball scouts), the two teams ultimately reached an amicable settlement. Radja went back to Yugoslavia to finish the 1989–90 season in Split, and the Celtics bought out his contract effective June 1, 1990.

39.
Some Shorties

1. When asked if I was scared to go to Medellín, Columbia, for depositions in a case because of the spree of kidnappings there, I replied, "No, lawyers don't bring much on the open market."

2. In 1989, with a straight face, the lawyer in open court said that his client, a former dealer of hallucinogenic drugs, had not violated probation because the nineteen pounds of marijuana found at his home was for personal consumption—pot was his drug of choice.

3. The famous rapper was taken out of the police cruiser when we got to the precinct and the handcuffs were taken off his hands before he posed for pictures with six different officers, one at a time.

4. The waiting room at Estefan Enterprises in Miami had a ten-foot-long rectangular glass table covered with fifty or sixty magazines with Gloria's picture on the front cover. The interior decorator was overpaid.

5. The client's pilot turned to me in the four-seater Cessna airplane, and with a jovial disposition said that his pilot license renewal test had gone "a little astray" when he overshot the runway and made a water landing. At 20,000 feet he said, "But you are safe with me."

6. On a trip to India visiting a client, the hired driver sped around the circular mountain in Rajasthan not slowing down for the goat herder with his wares. Three goats thudded against the car's front bumper and flew into the air in what seemed like slow motion. As he sped away, the goat herder raised his staff in a menacing way. Turning to me, in a thick accent the driver said, "Bad day to be a goat."

7. Numerous copyright applications are filed in Washington each

year attributing authorship to "God." The Copyright Office's position: a copyright cannot be owned by a deity.

8. The NBA star settled the case for less than the cost he would have incurred to rent a Lear jet to take him to the East Coast from California and return home thereafter.

9. When asked by Nina Simone's daughter Simone to represent her mother, I learned she was performing on Broadway in *Evita*. I asked Simone if she had a big part in the show, she turned to me and deadpanned, "I'm Evita."

10. Having successfully obtained a dismissal of a frivolous case brought against my client and its indemnitee, PepsiCo, I thought it advisable to pitch PepsiCo for additional legal work. After months of communications with PepsiCo's in-house attorneys, I finally landed a lunch with two of them in Purchase, New York. We met at Hamburger Heaven, a restaurant they selected. After a brief discussion about my law practice, the waitress took our order. I asked for a Coke. The lawyers I met with never called me again.

11. The Swedish client who had been a pawn in a multi-million-dollar Ponzi scheme wrote me and said, "The fortune teller says that you Brian are doing a very good job and will ultimately find the money."

12. The president and majority shareholder of a nationally distributed popular magazine, during a federal court-ordered mediation, turned to the magistrate judge who was trying to settle the case and said, "I am angry at you, but I won't kick you out of the room."

13. When introduced for the first time to my client, Greg Allman, backstage at the Beacon Theatre in New York while he was engaged in a heavy conversation with Dr. John, what brilliant things did I have to say? Absolutely nothing.

14. A great disappointment: not being able to depose Frank "The

Animal" Bialowas, a former American Hockey League enforcer who fought better than he scored.

15. The consummate rocker remarked, "I am a musician, but my girlfriend has a proper job."

16. The client looked me straight in the eyes and said, "I may be stupid, but I'm not stupid."

17. When a gorilla activates the shutter on a photographer's camera and takes a selfie, is the image copyrightable? And if so, by whom? The United States Copyright Office in August of 2014 said, "No." To be copyrightable the work must be the creation of a human being. For all of you who own elephants who can paint murals, you are out of luck.

40.
Great Names and Phone Messages

Some Unusual Band Names
(with whom I have interacted or represented)

Fun Lovin' Criminals

Anthrax

Twisted Sister

Trick Daddy

Grand Master Flash

LL Cool J ("Ladies Love Cool J")

The Cycle Sluts From Hell

The Young Rascals

The Gipsy Kings

The Jerky Boys

Earache Records

Joe

Allstar

Twista

Between the Buried & Me

The Cheetah Girls

Question Mark

The Velvet Underground

Beloved

Orange Juice Jones

Black Sheep

The Misfits

Shabba Ranks

The Underbellies

Pharaoh Munch

Gotye

Phone Messages

Big Chuck (six foot six, 345 pounds and growing):

Leave a message when you hear the beep and if I don't get back to you, let that be a message to you.

Additional Chuckisms:

What you don't see with your eyes, don't invent with your tongue.

What others think about you is none of your Bizness.

Recorded Message by a Member of Anthrax

I can't get to the phone right now because I don't know where it is.

It may be under the bed

in the bathroom

in the car

in the drum riser

on the plane

in the hotel room

When I find it, I will try to get back to you.

Interview Questions by Potential Clients over the Phone

1. Are you married? Do you have a mistress? I just want you to know before we get started that I have never faked an orgasm, so you can trust the things I say. What sign are you? What color are your eyes?

2. Can you take my case? Nobody else will.

3. I don't have money to pay you, but I am a nice guy. Can you take my case?

4. You're a Leo, you have my vote.

5. Are you tougher than the lawyer on the other side?

6. Will you fight the fight for me?

7. What is your winning percentage?

Phone Interviews

"Brian Caplan here."

"Question Mark here."

"Who?"

"Question Mark."

"What's a Question Mark?"

"Me. I'm a Question Mark."

"What's that mean?"

"Have you heard my '96 Tears?'"

"No. What's that?"

"A song I did in the 1960s with my group the Mysterions."

"Have not heard it, at least by the name of it, but maybe if I heard it I would know it."

"Can you help me?"

"I don't know, can I?"

[pause] "Hello, this is Grand Master Flash here."

"Who?"

"Grand Master Flash."

"What do I call you? Grand Master, Master Flash, or something else?"

"Flash will work."

41.
Crazy Claims

1. The rock 'n' roll fan who claimed he became hearing-impaired as a result of attending a concert. He asked the court reporter to reread the first question at his deposition. The question was, "What is your name?"

2. A dispute arose between the music publisher, owned by the aunt of the songwriter, and her nephew. She claimed one hundred thousand dollars in cash was in the brown paper bag given to her nephew. He said it was less than twenty-five thousand dollars.

3. The rapper (L'il Wayne) who didn't show up at his second court-ordered deposition said he was too tired from the party the night before.

4. The Run DMC concertgoer who claimed he was stabbed with an icepick smuggled into the venue and complained that with his injuries he could only play full-court basketball three times a week instead of five.

5. The alternative rock band member performing in Houston, Texas, was on his back being tossed around in a mosh pit and an adoring fan grabbed and held on to his testicles. The name of the officer that arrested him for striking the woman to get free and save his privates, Detective Booker. Question: Why did he book him and not her?

6. The older woman claimed that her image was used without her authority on the front page of a popular magazine. It was a photo of a young woman wearing a beautiful white and pink gown in a rowboat on a picturesque lake with weeping willow trees. When asked, "Were you ever in that boat?" she replied, "No." When asked, "Were you ever in that dress?" she replied, "No." When asked, "Did you ever wear that hat?" she replied, "No." When asked, "Doesn't that woman

in the photo look a lot younger than you?" she replied: "I was a lot younger then." "If you were never in that boat, never in that dress, and never wore that hat, what makes you think the image is you?" She answered, "They superimposed my face onto someone else's body and placed it on the boat. These things happen all the time."

7. The man in the New Orleans café heard me say that I was an attorney. He asked if he might have a moment of my time. He looked me straight in the eyes as if he was trying to read me and asked if I was spiritual and believed in supernatural forces. I told the man that I believe that certain events defy explanation. He then told me that he had two guardian angels. I told him I wished I had one and he was lucky. He said that one of his guardian angels was a public figure during her lifetime, and that both of them watch over and protect him. Without telling me who the deceased star was, the gentleman asked if I could help clear her name as she had been falsely accused of wrongdoing during her lifetime. I dissuaded him from contacting the media in the belief that no credible newspaper would give his story credence and he would be ridiculed. I suggested that a private investigator would be better than I would at uncovering the truth and removing any public stigma attached to her life. The man left with valuable but free advice.

42.
Some Rap Stories

1. The rapper was over six foot three and weighed almost twice as much as I. He was being charged with rape in Nassau County, New York. Our defense was that there had been consensual intercourse. The complainant had no bruises on her body, no ripped clothing, and had gone to a hotel room with my client after he performed at a concert. The next morning he had paid for a car service to take her home.

The Mike Tyson–Desiree Washington rape case was years away. Even though my client was claiming a consensual relationship existed, the prosecutor wanted DNA samples from him to compare to the semen retrieved from the claimant. A date was set for my client to submit to a blood test at the Nassau County District Attorney's office in Mineola.

The rapper was nervous to give blood as he was scared of needles, and asked me to pick him up at his home. We drove to Mineola and I assured him that everything would be all right. When we arrived at the D.A.'s office, a number of police officers posed with my client before he was processed. When the time came for the blood test, I was asked to stay by his side. Lucky I was because he fainted and went down like a ton of bricks and I became a brick catcher. I was sworn to secrecy to never tell anyone what happened.

2. The rapper didn't pay for the legal services I rendered. My firm sued to recover our legal fees. The rapper's father was deposed and said, "I go through lawyers like underwear. When they are dirty and used up, I throw them away."

3. When the famous rap producer came to my office to sign his settlement papers resolving the third paternity suit against him, I gave him a box of Trojans on his way out.

43.
Deposition Q & As

Trick Daddy, Rapper

Q. How did you get your name?

A. My momma was a hoe. My daddy was a pimp. Out I came
... Trick Daddy.

Russell Simmons, Music Impresario

Q. What did you do to deserve executive producer credit on the
album?

A. I ordered the fucking sandwiches.

Member of Black Uhuru

Q. Do you smoke marijuana on a regular basis?

A. Hey mon, what I do in my spare time is my business.

Lou Reed

Q. Is that your signature on the 1967 recording agreement?

A. I don't know.

Plaintiff in a Copyright Infringement Case

Q. Did the LSD ever affect your memory?

A. I don't remember.

Police Officer in a Hearing to Suppress Evidence

Q. Since the door was closed, how did you know what was going
on on the other side?

A. I'm a cop.

Rodney Dangerfield

Q. What do you do for a living?

A. I am a comedian. I make people laugh? Get it?

Jeff Timons, a member of 98 Degrees

Q. Is now a good time for a break?

A. Yes, I need to have a Tension Tamer tea.

Shaggy, whose hit single was "It Wasn't Me."

Q. Before I ask any other questions, I need to know one thing—was it you?

A. It wasn't me, mon.

Charles Smith, a member of Kool & The Gang

Q. How was the song created?

A. There were seven or eight of us in a room and people were throwing out ideas. Da-da-da, do-do-do, dee-dee-dee.

The court reporter interjects: How do you spell that?

A. Da-da-da. D, A, D, A, D, A. Do-Do-Do. D, O, D, O, D, O. Dee-dee-dee. D, E, E, D, E, E, D, E, E.

Plaintiff in a Copyright Infringement Case

Q. How did you come up with the idea for the song?

A. I got laid and smoked a joint. It was inspirational.

Another Plaintiff in Another Copyright Infringement Case

Q. Can you describe the similarities in the two songs?

A. Boy meets girl. Boy falls in love with girl. Boy and girl break up. Boy and girl get back together.

George Lang, Former Owner of Café Des Artistes, NYC/Author
of *You Don't Know the Truffles I've Seen*

Q. Exhibit A is the book you wrote and it notes on the jacket
cover that it was written by George Lang, Restaurateur, Raconteur,
Extraordinaire. Who came up with those lines to describe you?

A. George Lang did of course.

Q. Are all facts set forth in the book accurate and true?

A. George Lang does not lie.

The Owner of One of Many Concrete Companies in New York
Sued by the Attorney General's Office for Price-Fixing in Connection with the Construction of the Jacob Javits Center

Q. Sir, I am placing before you a series of checks payable to P.
Cash totaling 1.85 million dollars and ask you, sir, do you have any
employees by that name?

A. You mean Petty Cash?

Q. Does he work for you?

A. No, I don't think we have a guy on the payroll named Petty
Cash, but maybe we do.

The Road Manager for Run DMC in the Late 1980s.

Q. Why did Run DMC provide metal detectors to the Nassau
Coliseum?

A. To stop people from bringing in cameras, tape recorders, and
ice picks.

44.
Where's Herb?

In 1986, "Where's Herb?" was a popular television advertising campaign for Burger King. The commercials featured a character named Herb, who was identified as an individual who had never eaten at Burger King in his entire life. If a fan of Burger King were to actually find Herb, he or she would win a prize.

Our law firm represented a Herb of a different ilk. Herb G. was sixty-eight years old with gray scraggily hair, timid blue eyes, and an appearance like an elderly uncle or grandfather you wanted to embrace. At five foot five and 140 pounds when soaking wet, he was soft-spoken, and his syncopated speech pattern almost sounded melodic. Herb looked as harmless as could be. His rap sheet told a different story.

Herb's criminal accomplishments spanned more than fifty years and covered a broad range of social transgressions. From age eighteen on, he did one thing and only one thing quite well: pulling a scam. His rap sheet was seven pages long, three to four convictions to a page. Herb was a serial offender, who never met a police officer, investigator, prosecutor, or judge he could call his friend. Ponzi schemes, embezzlements, frauds, defalcations, criminal impersonations, filing false business records, posing as a banker, an insurance broker, or realtor, Herb was truly a jack of all trades.

Herb's latest day of reckoning was in December 1986, almost eighteen months after his arrest. His sentencing was before the imperious federal court judge Richard Owen from the Southern District of New York, a disciplinarian with no sense of humor and a track record of handing out stiff sentences to repeat offenders.

Herb's flavor-of-the-month scheme had taken a terribly wrong turn. Having pretended to be an agent for the Union Label Life Insurance Company, Herb needed to find his mark. He found his latest fall guys in Cincinnati, Ohio, a consortium interested in obtaining a 110 million dollar construction loan to build a shopping center. Only too eager to help in any way he could, Herb convinced his dupes that the Union Label Life Insurance Company could fund the loan, subject to due diligence on the consortium, filling out the loan paperwork and providing a 1 percent refundable good faith payment. Herb instructed the Ohio contingent to make the 1.1 million-dollar check payable to U.L.L.I.C.O. and he would take care of the rest.

After setting up the U.L.L.I.C.O bank account as the "president" of U.L.L.I.C.O, Herb deposited the 1.1 million dollars into the account. A week later Herb had control of the funds and off to Atlantic City he went. As bad a gambler as he was a criminal, Herb rapidly lost his bankroll. The million-dollar stake that he hoped to return after he doubled it at the tables was now gone. It was only a matter of time before the law caught up with Herb yet again.

In 1986, there were no mandated federal court sentencing guidelines, which meant that a trial judge had significant discretion handing out sentences. Herb was likely looking at eight to twelve years and restitution given his criminal history and the severity of the new offenses charged against him. The feel in a courtroom during a sentencing is hard to describe. It is anxious and serious, where too much is at stake. A proclamation from a judge is followed by a loss of liberty for a criminal defendant, the exact term of which is about to be decided.

The air in Judge Owen's courtroom was heavy. It was hard to breathe. A number of hearts in the room were racing. The prosecutor sat at the table on my left. My mentor Mark Arisohn and Herb sat at the defendant's table on the right. We all rose when Judge Owen entered.

Since Herb was pleading guilty to three counts of mail fraud, he needed to stand and make an allocution admitting to the underlying facts of the offense to which he was pleading guilty. The United States Attorney's office had agreed not to take a position on sentencing and to simply leave it in the judge's discretion. Following Herb's factual admission about his fraudulent scheme and its aftermath, Mark stood to give his presentencing presentation. During a speech that spanned more than thirty-five minutes, Mark gave an impassioned offering in an attempt to humanize Herb to the court.

Herb had made some mistakes in his life, but he was basically a good, decent man who could ultimately be an asset to society.

Herb appreciated the severity of his wrong doing and would not be led astray again.

Herb was not the same man today as the one who was arrested over eighteen months ago.

As a caring human being, Herb would routinely engage in meaningful conversations with Mark's young son when he called Mark's home.

Herb would provide complete restitution over time to those he had taken advantage of. Herb wanted to make amends.

There was a moment of silence in the courtroom when Mark finished. Everyone had an opportunity to catch their breath.

Judge Owen broke the silence.

"Herb G., do you have anything to say for yourself." Herb responded meekly, "No, Your Honor." Judge Owen deliberated and formed his thoughts. "Mr. G., you have a very good lawyer and he almost fooled me."

Judge Owen spoke in an authoritative voice with stern tones. He was not going to leave any doubt as to the point of his message.

Herb listened intently as the judge dissected his life, compared him to a blood-sucking parasite that had no worthwhile attributes and reflected on Herb's repeat-offender status. As Herb was being demonized, he started to break out into a cold sweat standing at the defense table.

Judge Owen continued. He talked about his discretion at the sentencing stage of the proceeding, but admonished Herb that each time he had gotten a "second chance," and there had been many of them, another victim had fallen prey to Herb. Like an aria in an opera reaching its crescendo, Judge Owen's voice reached its height of intensity just before he announced Herb's sentence.

As Judge Owen proclaimed that Herb would do six years in a federal penitentiary, Herb grabbed his chest and fell to the ground in a heap. Within minutes the courtroom was filled with EMS workers. An oxygen mask was put on Herb's head, but the air valve was not turned on as Herb actually started to turn blue.

With the ensuing chaos, Judge Owen left the bench and his courtroom.

The EMS team transported Herb to the Beekman Downtown Medical Center where he was held for observation for forty-eight hours.

Mark Arisohn wrote the court and the prosecutor giving them notice that Herb was scheduled to have an angioplasty a few weeks down the road.

The time for the angioplasty came and went. Neither the court nor the prosecutor followed up with respect to a surrender date at which time Herb G. would start serving his sentence of six years at a federal penitentiary.

During the next six months, I routinely told Mark that we needed to hope that neither Judge Owen nor the prosecutor ever watches the "Where's Herb" commercial for Burger King.

Herb G. never served his six-year sentence. Judge Owen forgot about him

The prosecutor forgot about him.

Herb G. lived another eleven years.

Three years later he married an attractive young Polish woman, thirty-five years his junior.

When Herb ultimately passed, his young wife came to our office about a week later and asked Mark where the "money had been stashed." She had been told by Herb that Mark knew the whereabouts of his nest egg.

Mark told her the truth.

There was no money.

Herb's widow was the last victim of his fraud. He just couldn't help himself.

45

A Lack of Appreciation
for Modern Art

Conrad Janis and Carroll Janis were the sons of Sidney Janis, a renowned New York City-based art dealer from 1948 through the late 1960s. During the 1950s, he became the dealer for Jackson Pollack, Arshile Gorky, Willem de Kooning, Mark Rothko, Franz Kline, and many others. Following the death of Sidney Janis in 1989, Conrad, an actor who among other things portrayed Mindy's father on *Mork & Mindy*, and Carroll Janis, a full-time art dealer, co-owned the Sidney Janis Gallery on West 57th Street and were partners in many businesses that owned significant twentieth-century artwork. During the late 1990s, I represented Conrad in a series of cases and disputes with his brother. Conrad was a warm, engaging man who could charm you over a glass of wine and a story.

Unfortunately, one of the byproducts of the dispute between Conrad and his brother was the closing of the gallery, which had been their father's legacy. On one occasion while I attended a meeting at the gallery, I noticed three sculptures sitting on a heating vent by a window overlooking 57th Street. The first piece was a combination of large metal nuts and bolts which had been soldered together to create an abstract form. The second piece was about fourteen inches tall, made of metal, and resembled a small totem pole. The third piece looked like a bronze football that had been dropped on a flat surface when it was in molten form, causing a flat side on an otherwise oval cylindrical surface. It was mounted on a nondescript base.

A gallery employee asked me what I thought of the three works, which appeared to be almost discarded, not encased or protected, simply loose, just sitting there. As an art neophyte I said the three pieces really didn't do anything for me and I wouldn't have purchased any of them if I saw them at a flea market.

The gallery employee said that the first work was done by Eduardo Chillida, a Spanish Basque sculptor, and the combination of nuts and bolts was worth seventy thousand dollars. The second piece, a combination of little mounted metal heads, was created by the sculptor, painter, and poet Jean Arp. Its price tag was seven hundred and fifty thousand dollars. My jaw dropped further. I thought to myself that I should rethink what to buy at flea markets. Now it was time for the pièce de résistance. The third sculpture, the football that didn't make it to the NFL was formed by Constantin Brancusi, a Romanian sculptor who pursued his career in France and is known as the father of twentieth-century modern sculpture. The value of this piece, I was told, was 1.8 million dollars.

I learned a valuable lesson. Do not opine on subject matters you know little about.

46.
Nobody Beats the Biz

Biz Markie, a successful rapper from the late '80s and early '90s, was a large teddy bear of a man. He was soft spoken and kind. His 1989 single "Just a Friend" became an American Top 10 hit. During the few years that I represented him, our interactions were always cordial and pleasant.

As with many rappers then and now, they wear their share of bling. It was 3:30 in the morning when the call came in from Biz during the winter of 1990. Biz had just flown from New York to LAX airport, and when he had woken from his sleep he discovered that his gold knuckles with inlaid diamonds had been taken off his hand by a very brave and daring soul. Biz was talking a mile a minute in a panic as I was trying to decipher what he wanted me to do three thousand miles away. Ultimately, I had to break it to him gently that it was impossible for me to obtain a court order in ten minutes requiring everybody on his plane to be strip searched before debarkation at the airport. Biz understood but was not happy with my answer.

47.
A Made Man

As a member of the Genovese crime family, Angelo had worked his way up over the years. By the age of fifty, his devotion to the family proven, he was bestowed with the honor of being "made." Unlike the "untouchables" of India, he was untouchable in a very different way. With tentacles stretching into the carting and construction industries, food services, protection, gambling, and prostitution, he was a family man in more ways than one. Angelo had seven children and fifteen grandchildren.

Every Sunday, Angelo, his wife Rosa, and their extended family would go to church. It was a ritual that Angelo could not miss. Holding Rosa's hand and checking his watch on a regular basis, Angelo routinely missed the homily recited by Father Ryan as his mind was elsewhere. Religion to Angelo meant family and tradition. Angelo was only half present at the masses. His mind was filled with football, baseball, and basketball games most Sundays, depending on what time of year it was. While he didn't need to pray at church that his Sunday selections would win, he wanted to be out of church and by a TV set by post time, one p.m. The distraction of gambling on a game, whether it was a two hundred dollar or ten thousand dollar wager, was a welcome relief from his responsibilities as a family man, an organized crime family man, or a businessman. Whether he won or lost was less important than the opportunity to drift away, which Angelo did on a regular basis.

48.
Taking on the Archdiocese of New York

It is not too often that a lawsuit makes the front-page lead story of both the *New York Post* and the *Daily News*. But when you alleged that an ordained priest of the Roman Catholic Church swindled an elderly woman out of four hundred and ninety thousand dollars before she died, and the Archdiocese of New York claimed the priest was "an independent contractor," and is not responsible for the wayward priest's conduct, you get some attention. The headlines read: "Father Flim Flam" and "Let U$ Prey."

Rose Cale was eighty-eight years old and had never been married when she passed in 2003. She was a devout Catholic parishioner who lived for two things: the Catholic Church and her brother Frank, with whom she had lived her entire life. During the last six years of her life, Rose was a regular parishioner at the Church of St. John the Martyr located on East 71st Street in Manhattan and attended mass almost every day. Monsignor John Woolsey, the trusted spiritual leader of the parish, performed mass at the church during this time frame.

From 1997 to 2003 Rose Cale and Monsignor Woolsey developed a close personal relationship. Rose confided in Monsignor Woolsey and he gave her spiritual guidance as they talked about the role of God in her life. Rose received holy communion from Woolsey, who also heard Rose's confessions and absolved her of any sins or transgressions that she believed she may have committed. Over time, Woolsey used his relationship of trust and confidence over Rose to induce her to give him one hundred thousand dollars to buy a condominium on the Jersey Shore and almost four hundred thousand dollars in stock. During these same six years, Rose was prodded into donating an additional tow hundred and forty-one thousand dollars directly to the church.

When a messenger of God asks you to do something, how do you say no?

Following Rose's death, I was retained by her estate to pursue claims against both Woolsey and those superiors at the Archdiocese who dictated his fate. The Archdiocese did their best to absolve themselves of any responsibility for Woolsey's actions.

Accordingly, the Estate of Rose Cale sued the Archdiocese of New York and Monsignor Woolsey in July 2004. Two claims were brought against Woolsey, one for "rescission based upon undue influence" (i.e., he had gotten Ms. Cale to make gifts to him based upon his power over her) and fraud as to her contributions directly to the church, which were believed to have been usurped in whole or in part by Woolsey. The two claims against the Archdiocese were for agency liability, which meant that the Archdiocese was responsible for Woolsey's conduct since it controls his activities, and negligence because it did not adequately supervise him even though the Archdiocese knew he was paid very little and routinely ran church fund drives involving significant sums donated from parishioners.

Since Monsignor Woolsey had squandered most, if not all, of his money living the high life, the case would only have legs if the claims against the Archdiocese were sustainable. The primary issue to be decided by the court was whether it was reasonably foreseeable, based upon the scope of a priest's duties and responsibilities, that a priest would use his position of trust and confidence over his parishioners to benefit himself financially to their detriment. While the Supreme Court of the State of New York, which is a lower court, ruled in our favor, the Appellate Division, New York's intermediate appellate court, ruled against the Cale estate, dismissing the claims against the Archdiocese.

As a direct result of the notoriety surrounding our case filing, the Archdiocese did a careful examination of the books and records of Woolsey's Upper East Side church and found that 837,000 dollars in church funds were transferred without authorization to Monsignor Woolsey's personal account and an additional two hundred and seventy thousand dollars was missing. Woolsey was indicted by the Manhattan District Attorney's office in 2004 and ultimately pled guilty in 2006 to stealing hundreds of thousands of dollars from the church. He was sentenced to one to four years in prison and was required to pay two hundred thousand dollars back to his former parish. During a jailhouse interview given to the *Daily News*, Woolsey confessed that he had an "addiction" and couldn't control his desire to buy designer clothes and Rolex watches, and go on expensive golfing trips.

At the end of the day, due to the Archdiocese's recovery from Woolsey, Woolsey had no assets left to satisfy the claims of the Estate of Rose Cale. This was a clear case of the Archdiocese failing to do the "right thing." They replenished their account and forsook the estate of their parishioner.

While I was disillusioned by the church's actions, the conduct did not sway my personal belief that the Church's overall moral teachings had value.

49.
Rolling with Some Stones

While an associate at Parcher Arisohn & Hayes in the mid- to late-1980s, one of the firm's clients was the Rolling Stones. We represented the band in connection with litigation and did personal work for some of its individual members, including Mick Jagger and Keith Richards, who would, on occasion, drop by the office. Mick was all business and a bit aloof. Keith was extremely friendly and would sometimes stop into the individual lawyer offices of our seven-person firm and say hello.

On one occasion Keith popped his head into my office and invited me to a party he and his wife Patti Hansen were throwing. How could I say no? The party was on a Thursday night at a swank club in lower Manhattan off of Hudson Street. My date for the evening at the last minute cancelled so I went by myself. Some people are good at striking up conversations with strangers. I am not. When I got to the party, I was a bit uneasy. I did not know anyone and most people came in couples. Keith was nowhere to be seen. After my third drink on an empty stomach, and some bantering with an attractive but vapid hairdresser, I was feeling no pain.

When Keith sauntered in, I made a beeline for him and said, "You can relax now your legal counsel is here." Keith looked at me and responded in his British accent, "I feel better already." Keith spent the next twenty minutes talking to me like I was his brother. He discussed his married life, the rigors of touring, recording a new album with Mick and the differences of opinion they would have during the process. You had to be there to believe it, as I surely didn't. Just as we were running out of things to talk about (as I didn't think the New York

Yankees or the Civil War would interest Keith), Patti arrived at the party. Keith saw her, hugged me and said, "I gotta go, the wife's here." Since nobody else present could fascinate me as much as Keith, I left without any fanfare.

In 1988, I was given an assignment to accompany the Charlie Watts Jazz band on a tour date in Hartford, Connecticut. The orchestra consisted of more than twenty-five musicians from the UK and Charlie. As many of these seasoned musicians were boisterous and enjoyed a drink here and there, it was my job to make sure that nobody got into any mischief. Since I was twenty-seven at the time and most if not all of the band members were forty-five to sixty, it was curious that I was minding them. Early on a Saturday morning, I met Charlie's tour manager who escorted me to the bus used for the tour. She ushered me down the aisle and introduced me one-by-one to all the guys. I was the lawyer who would "help keep them out of trouble." Eventually, Charlie showed up, said a quick hello, and sat by himself as the bus left for Hartford.

During the bus ride, followed by the rehearsals, Charlie had very little to say. It was clear that he took his music very seriously and was not a particularly talkative sort. Despite a significant amount of beer intake and an occasional swig taken from a whiskey flask, the band members behaved themselves. I got to spend the day and night listening to excellent jazz. The bus ride back to New York was filled with noise and laughter. When we got back in the wee hours of the morning, I felt satisfied that nobody was arrested on my watch.

50.
Catch Me If You Can

As an accountant in the music industry once said, "Nobody has ever done an audit of a major record or publishing company in the music industry and found that they were overpaid." Recording artists and songwriters customarily get accounted to for royalties twice a year, ninety days after each six-month calendar interval ending June 30th and December 31st. To understand the royalty provisions in a standard recording agreement you would need a team of professionals akin to a think tank composed of a soothsayer, a man of the cloth, an English teacher, an accountant, and a lawyer. The soothsayer would look into a crystal ball and tell you that the band is going to "get screwed." The man of the cloth would pray for the band's salvation and a royalty check sufficient to pay for their living expenses between gigs. The English teacher would attempt to read through the recording agreement and interpret its verbiage giving the language "plain meaning." The accountant would crunch the numbers and verify the amount of underpayments made by the record label. And the lawyer would try to be the band's enforcer if enough money was at issue.

Modern publishing agreements for songwriters are far easier to interpret and generally more transparent than recording agreements, and they contain fewer provisions authorizing deductions in the accounting process, such as the myriad costs associated with recording, releasing, and promoting a record album.

What both record companies and music publishers have in common is that they have little incentive to accurately account for the money due to their recording artists and songwriters. They bank on the fact that when they underpay the parties that contract with them, such underpayments will generally be discovered only by an auditor hired by the recording artist/songwriter at significant expense (only justified if a significant royalty income stream exists). Accordingly, the little guy, who does not earn over a hundred thousand dollars in royalties per year, has little incentive to pay for an audit. Where audits are performed on behalf of successful artists and songwriters, and not amicably resolved, lawyers, at an additional expense, need to be retained. If a lawsuit is brought against a record label or music publisher, neither the auditor's nor lawyer's fees are generally recoverable by the plaintiff. Moreover, short of a trial court judgment, which is rare in an audit dispute, record and publishing companies *never* pay any interest on audit claims.

Ask yourself why then would a record company and publishing company ever give its recording artists and songwriters accurate and complete accountings when they know it will cost them a lot of money to catch them? They know that many can't afford high-priced accountants and lawyers. They know that they have the resources to fight you and they know they will never pay you interest on your claim.

In New York, the statute of limitations, the time within which you must start a lawsuit or otherwise lose your right to do so, is six years for breach of contract cases. The record companies and music publishers are so concerned with making sure they accurately account for royalties to their bands and songwriters that they include an "incontestability clause" in their contracts that states that any royalty statements not challenged within a much shorter time frame than the six years (usually one to three years) are deemed to be correct and incontestable at the end of such period. There is usually an additional "time to sue" provision, which states that any lawsuit relating to a challenged royalty statement must be brought within a specified time frame or the right to do so is lost.

You might be surprised to learn that many legacy/Top 40 acts routinely conduct audits every two years and recover large sums of money from record companies and publishers, which ultimately has no impact upon their ongoing relationship with these entities. Even in these situations, the audits are settled on a lump-sum basis, with no individual line-item claim being agreed to, which might otherwise have a precedential effect on other cases, and the record/publishing company requires a confidentiality provision so that the terms of the settlement are not disclosed to others.

While it may appear that the deck is stacked against everybody but the superstars, every once in a while the little guy can pull a rabbit out of his hat. So was the case with Gary Puckett, the lead singer in the iconic band "Gary Puckett and the Union Gap" from the late 1960s.

Gary, a kind, soft-spoken, and spiritual man with an amazing voice, gave us "Young Girl," "Woman, Woman," and "Lady Will-power." He and the Union Gap formed one of the most successful bands of the 1960s, selling more records than the Beatles in 1968.

In 1997, Gary, through an auditing firm, did a "desktop" audit (a less comprehensive and cursory form of audit) of Sony Music, which revealed a claimed underpayment of approximately thirteen thousand dollars. Sony did not even respond to a demand for payment of this "trifle" sum. One of the line item claims in Gary's audit was based upon Sony Music's long-time practice of deducting 150 percent of any value added tax ("VAT") it paid in connection with the foreign sales of records embodying performances of Sony recording artists, even though the subject recording agreements only permitted Sony to deduct "all taxes" it actually paid when calculating record royalties.

Gary, in a selfless act, solely predicated on the principal of obtaining justice for the little guys against the 900-pound gorilla, agreed to serve as a class representative in a class action lawsuit against Sony to redress Sony's "blatant breach of contract." In order to maintain a class action one must show:

• the class is so numerous that joinder of all members is impracticable;

• there are questions of law or fact common to the class which predominate over any questions affecting only individual members;

• the claims of the representative parties are typical of the claims of the class;

• the representative party will fairly and adequately protect the interests of the class; and

• a class action is superior to other available methods for the fair and efficient adjudication of the controversy.

We filed our class action lawsuit against Sony Music in 1998. Sony's arrogant outside counsel brazenly told me and my cocounsel that we "would never get class certification" and, if we ever did, the attorney's fees that we would recover would not amount to anything more than fifty cents per hour. He was wrong on both counts.

Although it took almost four years of guerrilla warfare and a few casualties along the way, the court, in 2002, Justice Leland DeGrasse presiding, granted class certification status to the plaintiff class in *Gary Puckett, et al. v. Sony Music Entertainment*, Index No. 108802/98, finding that Gary Puckett and Robert Watson (his coplaintiff) were "appropriate class representatives to represent a class of some 1,500 recording artists and producers to whom Sony accounts for foreign record royalties . . ."

"Plaintiffs are arguing that Sony's alleged policy of reducing the royalty bases by 150 % of the relevant VAT is not a bargained for term, but rather a blanket policy that is in breach of plaintiffs' various contracts . . ."

". . . this experience is illustrative that the audit process is not as simple as Sony implies. The expense of the audit process would likely deter artists who could not be sure that they would recover any money, or sufficient money to justify the time, effort and expense of hiring outside professionals. By contrast, the class action is a useful mechanism for recovery of small amounts of damages distributed among a large group of people."

The *Puckett* decision represented the first time a court had certified a class action of recording artists and producers in the music industry. Since it is extremely difficult for anyone other than powerful, high-profile recording artists and producers to obtain legal redress against record companies due to the high costs of hiring attorneys and accountants, this decision was significant and paved the way for other such cases. Gary Puckett helped create a way for all recording artists and producers, regardless of their means or present popularity, to challenge the propriety of the royalty accountings that they are provided.

51.
The Bootlegger's Tale

Bootlegging, or the illegal sale of copyrighted or trademarked merchandise, is a multi-billion-dollar cottage industry. "Now you see me, now you don't" is especially apt to describe the bootlegger who gets his wares from underground factories usually in the United States or China, stores them in unmarked boxes in remote or illicit warehouses, then surreptitiously transports them to a sale site, sneaking away into the night. Bootlegging affects the garment, motion picture, music, and women's accessories industries, among others.

In the band merchandising business, bootlegging is exceptionally bad and difficult to combat. Annually, hundreds of thousands of counterfeit t-shirts are sold outside of concert arenas around the country. Bootleggers park their vehicles within close proximity to their target audience, usually with an entourage of accomplices, and sell their inferior-quality wares on the street when the concerts are over for a third or a quarter of the price that authorized merchandise sells for inside the concert venue.

There are two primary ways to fight bootlegging: one, obtain a federal court bootleg seizure order for a client allowing you to confiscate unlicensed merchandise sold in public areas; or two, use a confidential informant to obtain a court order to raid a factory or manufacturing facility known for making bootleg merchandise with federal marshals or designated private investigators.

From 1985 to 1990, my law firm was frequently engaged by Winterland Concessions Co., a San Francisco-based manufacturer of music industry t-shirts and a leader in that field, to go after the bad guys.

During Bruce Springsteen's "Born in the U.S.A." tour in 1985 we seized over forty thousand t-shirts in and around Giants Stadium in the Meadowlands alone. Upon approval from the court we were permitted to donate these shirts to the March of Dimes. Months later we received a batch of personally handwritten notes from Native American children living on reservations out West thanking Mr. Springsteen for the shirts bearing his likeness.

In another case, we were able to seize and search a vehicle used by Gene P., one of the biggest bootleggers of rock 'n' roll t-shirts in the country at the time. In the car were blank cotton shirts, bootleg t-shirts, and Mr. P.'s calendar and business records. The calendar identified music concerts around the country listing the city and venue where the concert was or had taken place, frequently listing two, three, or four different concerts on the same date. Included in Mr. P.'s business records were invoices from a cotton t-shirt manufacturer. We ultimately subpoenaed records from this manufacturer and ascertained that Mr. P. had purchased hundreds of thousands of blank t-shirts. We went to trial against Mr. P. as a repeat bootleg offender in federal court in Uniondale, Long Island. Rejecting Mr. P.'s contention that his calendar was used to pick concerts to take his son to and that he wore a lot of cotton t-shirts, the judge awarded Winterland a multi-million-dollar judgment against Mr. P. The formula for the damage calculation was: Winterland's market share percentage in the music t-shirt marketplace multiplied by the number of blank t-shirts Mr. P. had purchased during the relevant time frame multiplied by the average net revenue Winterland and its recording artist licensors received from the sale of each t-shirt.

In another case we handled, an individual caught bootlegging a few hundred t-shirts agreed to become our confidential informant and disclosed the existence of a manufacturing facility in Yonkers, New York, not too far from the Metro North train station there. Once we obtained court approval to enter the premises with federal marshals and designated off-duty court officers, we had to synchronize our raid. I felt like I was a member of Elliot Ness's Untouchables on the day of our adventure. Three large dark vehicles with a total of twelve men left the city headed for Yonkers. Our court order allowed us to enter the premises, search for evidence of bootlegging activity, and seize any counterfeit shirts as well as their means of production. Our target was located within a multifacility brick structure that was a few blocks long and contained plants, factories, and warehouse space. We were going in through the back where loading docks for truck pick-ups and deliveries took place.

With two lawyers and ten officers of the court, we approached. I had a number of copies of our court order to give to anyone we encountered so they would know we had the authority for our actions. With my support behind me, I walked through the unlocked rear door to the plant. A Spanish gentleman approached, and I identified our group, gave him a court order, and asked for him to point out the boss or owner. He could barely hear me as the noise from multiple presses going at once was almost deafening, so I had to lean over and yell by his left ear. He pointed across the expanse of an adjacent warehouse-sized room filled with presses, other heavy equipment and boxes, to a balding middle-aged Caucasian man with a quizzical look upon his face as he gazed at twelve strangers who had invaded his space. As a group of us walked toward him, while two marshals stayed at the door, we passed the end of one of the presses where finished product was being spit out onto a small conveyor. Right there before our eyes were warm shirts coming hot off the presses bearing the likeness of a Top 40 band signed to Winterland.

As I announced who we were and gave the owner a copy of our seizure order, dumbfounded, the owner could only say, "I guess you caught me with my pants down." That indeed we did. Over the course of the next two-and-a-half hours, we seized thousands of bootleg shirts, depicting multiple bands, and all the presses, leaving behind a fairly empty warehouse.

52.
Me Versus Larry Flynt
(Not Really)

I received a call from my client Ralph Mercado late on a Thursday night asking me if I was free to attend a property auction with him Friday morning. Ralph and his record label RMM Records had been clients of mine for years.

Ralph was a Latin music promoter who brought Latin jazz, merengue, and salsa concerts into Madison Square Garden and the United States starting in the 1960s. He managed performing artists, had the record label, and publishing company, and owned nightclubs and restaurants. In life he was a "player." Incredibly he got his start in the music industry by promoting "waistline parties" in apartment buildings, which were live music events where women were charged entrance fees based upon their waist size, the wider the woman, the higher the cover charge. Ultimately, he managed Celia Cruz and Tito Puente and discovered Marc Antony and La India whom he signed to his label. By the mid-1980s, Ralph had over a hundred Latin recording artists and performers either signed to management or his label. In 1991, *Billboard Magazine* identified Ralph as "the entrepreneur who took salsa from New York to the world." In the late 1990s when Marc Antony sought to leave RMM Records and move to Sony Music, Ralph engaged me to protect his interests. Following our lawsuit against both Marc Antony and Sony, Ralph was able to smile again.

Ralph and his driver picked me up in front of my office at ten a.m., and I was quickly told that we were going to a law office downtown to bid on a city-licensed strip club that had gone into bankruptcy.

Ralph and a "plumber" were partners in this potential acquisition, and I was to be the designated bidder at the auction. The facility at issue was located at 641 West 51st Street and had been there for years. When we walked into the offices it was buzzing with activity. Numerous people were registering to bid and handing over their two-hundred-thousand-dollar certified checks to satisfy their condition to demonstrate financial solvency to bid. These checks were to be returned to all but the winning bidder. The crowd was diverse. Businessmen in suits, women in tight dresses, unshaven guys in jeans, all types. Numerous factions filled the room and there were huddled "hush-hush" conversations taking place in every corner. Ralph handed in our certified check and we were off to the races. Like at Sotheby's and Christie's we were given a paddle with a number on it for bidding purposes. We were paddle number two.

After another twenty minutes of chatting it up, already given my instructions as to how high we would bid, the auction was close to starting. One of the bankruptcy attorneys at the firm stood and detailed the terms of the auction. All the personal property at the Stingray Facility was part of the transaction. Subject to appropriate background checks on the buyer, the liquor and cabaret licenses for the business, and the leasehold interest to the property (and what it entailed and what it didn't) would all go to the winning bidder. Last but not least, a list of liens on the property, which needed to be satisfied, were rattled off by the attorney.

Next, the auctioneer stood and explained the rules of the auction, none of which were out of the ordinary. There was a charged excitement in the air and I could feel my heart racing with anticipation. As people started moving in toward where the auctioneer was standing, two gentlemen who looked like bouncers in a strip club and were standing together caught my eye. Both over six feet tall, with large biceps not so well hidden under their blazers, they were a formidable sight.

I was directed to and did open the bidding at 2,520,000 dollars, twenty thousand dollars over the required opening bid. Bidders number one and number six joined the fray and before you knew it, we were at 3,370,000 dollars. One of the two designated bouncers holding paddle number three confidently and succinctly called out that he was raising the bid by 1.2 million dollars to 4,570,000 dollars. This tactic is known as an attempted "shut-out bid" where you try to scare your competition into submission. It almost worked. There was a distinct hush and shock that befell the crowd. The bid was separating the men from the boys. We were now past the high limit I had been given for the bidding. I looked to Ralph for guidance. He was standing with his plumber partner, who was dressed in dirty overalls. With his charismatic smile he looked at me and nodded his head to continue forward. I stated 4,670,000 dollars without reservation. Paddle number three moved the bid up by another one hundred thousand dollars. Back and forth we went by one hundred thousand dollars increments while the rest of the room watched in fascination as the two "players" continued. One was in the room in person and the other player had sent his designated tough guy agents. On we went, 5,370,000 dollars, 5,470,000 dollars, each time me looking to Ralph and getting the "nod." Finally, when I reached the 6,070,000 dollar-plateau I requested that the auctioneer give us a five-minute break so that I could consult with my clients (rather than just go with the nods). My request was granted.

I was convinced that there was an endless supply of money behind paddle number three. During the bidding process thus far the two goons were staring me down, apparently upset that I was costing their boss money, which somehow reflected poorly upon them. I expressed my beliefs to my team and received my final instructions on my bidding ceiling.

We went back to work, 6,170,000 dollars from them. 6,270,000 dollars from me. We continued until I got to my limit and bid 6,670,000 dollars. When one of the big boyz said 6,770,000 dollars, the auctioneer and the crowd looked to me for a response, but none was forthcoming. I looked one last time to Ralph and the smile was gone. He simply shook his head in defeat. The auctioneer yelled out fair warning: going once, going twice, gone . . . sold to paddle number three.

You can't win them all.

Within a year, Larry Flynt's Hustler Club opened at 641 West 51st Street.

53.
Swedish Due Process

Smoking marijuana is illegal in Sweden.

The call from the transactional attorney came in at 11:15 on a Friday night. His client was in the back of a police car in a small city in Sweden being driven to the police station charged with "Suspicion of being under the influence of narcotics."

I was able to call the Reggae Man and calm him down. I told him I would contact a Swedish attorney and that he should say nothing for now but call me when he arrived at the police station.

Through some quick investigation on my part, I learned that Swedish police have a right to request that a suspect submit to giving blood and urine samples and if you refuse, they can hold you for up to forty days in captivity.

Within forty-five minutes, I was back on the phone with the Reggae Man shortly before he was to be questioned by his investigators.

I then spoke with one of the officers who confirmed that I could participate or at least listen in to the interview process.

Like an arraignment, the Reggae Man was told he was being charged with being under the influence of narcotics and how did he plead?

He answered, "Not guilty."

The Reggae Man was then asked: Have you ever used narcotics?

I objected and said what falls within the category of narcotics and what relevance does the question of Reggae Man's history of narcotics use have to his short time in Sweden. The interrogator told me that if I interrupted again my line would be disconnected. I replied,

"That's easy for you to say five thousand miles from me."

The following questions were then asked and answered:

"When is the last time you used narcotics?"

"What did you use?"

"Have you used any narcotics since you have been in Sweden?"

"Have you taken any medication for health purposes?"

"If we obtained a positive urine sample, would you be able to explain why that happened?"

"Can you explain why you have certain symptoms consistent with drug use: bloodshot eyes, dilated pupils?"

"Is there any possibility that you could have inhaled cannabis today?"

"If the prosecutor finds you guilty today because of the results from the blood or urine sample test, are you willing to pay a fine?"

"Have you seen anybody smoke cannabis since you have been in Sweden?"

After answering all the questions to the satisfaction of the officer, the Reggae Man was released. I smoked a joint and went to bed.

54.
"Beloved"

In order to be an effective representative of a client, you need to be able to assess the client quickly, speak the client's language, and gain the client's respect from the inception of the relationship onward.

I received the call on a Wednesday, late in the afternoon. A.T. said that none of the litigation attorneys in his large national law firm were up to the task of meeting with "Beloved," a tough guy who just got out of prison after six-and-a-half years hard time. Beloved had legal issues that needed to be addressed and wanted a consult. A.T. asked if I would take the meeting. "No problem," I said without hesitation.

A.T. gave me the lowdown on Beloved. He had a second-grade education, couldn't read or write, but had dictated the lyrics to over a hundred rap songs into a recording device while in the joint. As a man of the street it was not likely that Beloved had used the legal system to his advantage on prior occasions. His only issue had been concern with survival. He now had contractual issues that needed analysis.

I was one of twenty-two partners in a sixty-lawyer law firm housed in spacious offices on Park Avenue with impressive décor and large conference rooms. Beloved and his posse of two arrived only twenty minutes late, record time for most urban performers. A tough guy wannabe he wasn't. He was the real McCoy and had the scars to prove it. Beloved was chiseled and resembled the Rock 'Em Sock 'Em robots of my youth. He had biceps the size of my calves, and each had multiple slash scars from prior encounters. Cutting two-thirds across his sturdy neck was another wound site that started from just under his left ear and traced the line of his lower jaw until it ended slightly right of his Adam's apple. I wanted to know what the other guy in the encounter looked like, but didn't ask.

Beloved wore dark reflective sunglasses to camouflage his eyes, a short-sleeve shirt cut off at the shoulders revealing his arsenal, and ripped jeans. He walked with swagger and determination. Beloved was clearly a leader, not a follower. His two corner men walked behind him and were engulfed by Beloved's shadow. Two gents he could devour for dinner if he so chose.

Instinctively, I walked straight to Beloved and shook his hand with as firm a handshake as I could muster, knowing that if I was soft he would know it and gain the upper hand. After exchanging pleasantries and introductions in my firm's reception area, the four of us moved into a large conference room. We sat around a large boardroom-type table with me strategically placed directly across from Beloved so that I could look him in the face when I was talking and making a point.

The meeting lasted almost two hours. Beloved told his story, and I was given a contract and some correspondence to review. I asked questions. Beloved's "boyz" tried to appear useful, but on those few occasions that they spoke, Beloved cut them off. "Shut the fuck up, I just want to hear from the lawyer."

Each time they snapped to attention, stopped talking midsentence, and rested their hands on the table, mum again.

During the meeting I talked the talk. I was as straight as I could be. I gave advice and explained my strategy for "fucking up" Beloved's adversary.

"This is how we can fuck them up. We will rip them a new asshole. They don't know who they're fucking with."

Beloved gradually felt comfortable and understood that I was adopting his battle as that of my own. He knew that on this occasion I could be his warrior.

My plan of attack fully developed and imparted to Beloved, he seemed to almost buy the idea that for once the law could work for a guy like him. He rose and said, "We're cool" as he walked to the conference room door. I scurried around the table, reached to shake his hand, and simultaneously blocked his exit. As he gave me a firm and pronounced grasp of the hand, I looked into his dark sunglasses and in a most serious tone said, "You can't leave yet!"

Bewildered, he asked, "Why?"

Without hesitating I replied, "You've been in here for almost two fucking hours wearing those damn sunglasses, and I have no fucking idea who I've been talking to because I haven't seen your eyes."

Beloved's "boyz" looked at me like I was crazy, tempting fate and had a death wish.

Beloved slowly reached up and took his glasses off, leaned his head forward so that his eyes were ten inches from mine and, staring straight at me, said, "You okay," shaking his head in approval. He strode out the door and his "boyz" followed.

Years later when I inquired of A.T. as to what ever happened to Beloved, I learned that he had been shot and killed in the Bronx only a few months after our meeting.

55.
Rick Ross "Gangsta Rapper"

True "gangsta" rappers have no incentive for the world to know that one day in the past they were correctional officers. It undermines their street cred. Such was the case with Rick Ross, one of Miami's finest. At six feet tall and 380 pounds, Ross was a menacing figure. He borrowed his name either intentionally or by accident from "Freeway Ricky Ross" a convicted kingpin drug dealer in California, who ultimately sued him for trademark infringement.

Ross was a big dude with big attitude. Many of his songs glorified violence, crime, and the life of a drug dealer. He carefully tailored his public image and persona, one inconsistent with being a correctional officer.

My client, Vlad Lubouny, popularly known as DJ Vlad, had an Internet website known as VladTV with millions of patrons, in which he published the latest gossip in the rap world. A story of interest was the ongoing rumor that Rick Ross, a member of the Maybach music cartel, was in fact a corrections officer at an earlier time in his life. Repeated denials of the "slanderous accusations" by Ross only highlighted the public's interest in the debate. Then the pictures surfaced. The choirboy was now a tough guy wannabe, a "gangsta rapper." Looking fairly fit and trim in a neat white with gray trim pressed correctional officer uniform and wearing a tie, Ross looked proud of his accomplishment at age nineteen. With Ross's photo going viral on the Internet (among those who had any interest in the subject), someone would have to pay for this blasphemy.

Ross, a subtle sort, texted Vlad: "Niggaz will learn Trilla." Trilla being the name of Mr. Ross's second album.

Ross then demanded a meeting with Vlad at the "Ozone Awards" in Houston, an event they both would be attending.

When Vlad and Ross ultimately met at a crowded conference center, Ross was surrounded by his posse, "Gunplay," "Jeter," and "Gucci," three scary guys with the manners of street thugs.

Upon seeing Vlad approaching, Ross authoritatively states, "We got beef."

After another minute of discussion, Ross appreciating Vlad's role as a pseudo journalist of events in the hip-hop world says, "You want something to print? You want me to give you something to print? You want me to give you . . ."

Vlad suddenly and unexpectedly gets shoved away from Ross by Gucci.

Jeter, lying in wait, coldcocks Vlad in the jaw as he is falling backward.

Gucci then throws a drink in Vlad's face.

Then Gunplay, wearing Ross's twenty-thousand-dollar gold medallion necklace around his neck, hits a defenseless Vlad with a bottle over his head.

With Vlad lying semiconscious and bloodied on the ground, Jeter hovers over Vlad and says, "Print that. Print that."

Ross, the director of the one-act play, then leaves the scene of the crime with his actors, his supporting cast in tow. The entourage leaves as an assembly together. They lumber together out of the room as a team that accomplished its mission.

A number of attendees at the Ozone Awards were in this gathering. Many had their cameras going, filming rappers doing "shout outs." As soon as Vlad's beating was completed, E Class, one of Ross's co-managers, a rather tall, muscular man wearing a "wife-beater" t-shirt, grabs every movie camera and video camcorder in sight and stomps on them, destroying any evidence they may have captured. He successfully wrestled away every recording device except one, which housed the video footage of the savage beating.

Vlad suffered trauma to his face, requiring twelve stitches, and nerve damage to his cheek, gums, and lip. Following my retention as DJ Vlad's attorney and the filing of a multi-million-dollar lawsuit against Rick Ross, Ross went on a radio interview campaign to tell his side of the story.

Angela Ye asked Ross if he tells people around him, "Let's try not to address things physically."

Ross responds, "If a nigga gets his head bust, he gets his head bust. Was I supposed to feel bad?"

He goes on to say, "If I would have put my hands on him he may have died. I may have gotten sued for one hundred million dollars."

In an interview with Funk Master Flex, Ross said, "But yeah, it was an unfortunate situation. This DJ they say was really big doing push-ups, looks something like Curley."

Flex asked Ross, "And he approached you?"

Ross responded chuckling, "I don't know. Did he approach me? My memory is faint. He looked like the elephant man or something. I think the guy needed four hundred stitches or something."

Never short on words, Ross also released a recording during the pendency of our lawsuit with lyrics directly targeted at DJ Vlad.

"For the record, pussy. Far from a C.O.

Steppin' out the shower smelling like a kilo.

Bustin' a pussy nigga's head.

You can sue me.

But play me like a pussy

You will never do me."

Ross clearly excelled in his poetry class at the university. Robert Frost, Emily Dickinson, Walt Whitman, and Edgar Allan Poe would all have been envious of Ross's ability to melodically string together phrases.

The four-day jury trial that took place in federal court in Manhattan in April 2010, had the air and feel of a criminal trial. Ross's entourage included his mother who sat by his side throughout the trial. Ross's bling was left at home.

Exhibit A in the case was the videotape of the brutal assault, which was played for the jury on numerous occasions, each time leaving the jurors wincing. Vlad methodically described his role in posting the pictures of Ross as a C.O., his communications with Ross leading up to their meeting, the attack upon him, and its long-term impact upon his life, both physically and psychologically.

During Ross's direct testimony he said he couldn't have had anything to do with the attack on Vlad because "DJs are the oxygen for recording artists."

However, during a rigorous cross-examination of Ross he ultimately acknowledged that right before the beating, Ross believed Vlad had it coming to him.

The jury was only out a few hours and returned a verdict against Ross for three hundred thousand dollars. Ross tweeted to his adoring public that he had been victorious in his court case because Vlad had been seeking one million dollars against him.

56.
Eric B. and Rakim

Eric B. and Rakim were a hip-hop duo from Long Island. Their first single, "Eric B. is President" was released in 1986, followed by their debut album *Paid in Full*, released in 1987, which put Eric B. and Rakim on the map as influential rap artists. During the late 1980s they engaged Parcher Arisohn & Hayes to represent them in a litigation with a record label. I was given the task of defending both Eric and Rakim during their respective depositions. Eric showed up for his, but Rakim was a no-show on two occasions, leaving me, opposing counsel, and a court reporter twiddling our thumbs in a conference room. Opposing counsel filed an application with the court seeking to strike our answer and enter a default judgment against Rakim or in the alternative sanction him for his conduct. The court set a hearing date requiring Rakim's presence. I told Rakim to be on time and dress conservatively for the hearing.

I arrived at court thirty minutes before our scheduled hearing. Rakim and his bodyguard showed up fifteen minutes later. The court building had not yet installed metal detectors, which made entering the building easier than it is today. While I was pleasantly surprised to see Rakim arrive early, I was chagrined to see that Rakim was wearing enough gold jewelry to drown a beaver. Searching the corridor to make sure that my opposing counsel was not yet present, I ushered Rakim and his bodyguard to a secluded area on the second floor. I told Rakim he needed to remove all the gold before the hearing or the sanction he would likely receive would be significantly greater. There were gold knuckles on his left hand, large gold rings on two fingers on his right hand, and enough gold necklaces that you couldn't see his chest. The word "bling" was not yet in our vocabulary, but Rakim, as a trendsetter, was ahead of the curve.

It literally took Rakim over five minutes to remove all the jewelry as his bodyguard cupped his hands and accepted the donation. What a sight it was. This huge bodyguard in a sports coat, wearing dark sunglasses, holding more than a pound of gold. I asked him to make himself scarce until the hearing was over.

Fortunately, the judge was in a good mood. He denied the application to strike our answer and ordered Rakim to pay a small fine for his transgressions. Rakim showed up for his next scheduled deposition date and was an excellent witness.

57.
Memphis Bleak,
a Jay Z Prodigy from the Hood

The year was 2004. My client was Memphis Bleak, a prodigy of Jay Z from the Marcy Projects in Bedford Stuyvesant, Brooklyn. Bleak's third album entitled M.A.D.E. contained a single called "Round Here." Three obscure members of a band in southern Florida, who had never released a record but had played in a few clubs in the Fort Lauderdale area, claimed that "Round Here" infringed upon their copyright in a song called "Around Here."

In a music copyright infringement case the plaintiff must prove that: (1) the defendant songwriter had "access" to the plaintiff's work, which means a reasonable opportunity to hear it, and (2) there is substantial similarity with respect to a copyrightable element found in each work. There are numerous defenses to claims of copyright infringement, including the defenses of: (a) independent creation; (b) lack of copyrightable subject matter; and (c) any similarities between the songs relate to trite or commonly used lyrics or musical note progressions. No lawyer should take on a copyright infringement case for a plaintiff without first engaging a musicologist to compare the two works at issue and do a survey of prior art to confirm that any similarities between the two works can't be found in other works.

I told the lawyer for the plaintiffs that neither Memphis Bleak nor T.I. nor Trick Daddy, two additional featured performers on the track, had ever heard the plaintiffs' song before or been to the clubs in Lauderdale where it may have been played, and any similarities between the two works involved trite or common place expressions ("Around Here" and "Round Here"). Nevertheless, the lawyer for the three Floridians decided to move forward with the case.

When it came time for Bleak's deposition, I flew down to Miami to meet him the day before to go over the facts with him and prepare him for how a deposition worked. I was told by his manager to meet Bleak at a restaurant at eight p.m. When I got there, loud music was playing in a party environment and I found Bleak with a smile on his face with two attractive, scantily clad women, one on each arm. Bleak asked me what he needed to know for the next day, and I politely told him we would need to be alone to prepare. He looked at me like I was crazy to suggest he let go of his two companions and said, "No way. Not now." After some negotiation between Bleak, his manager, and me, it became, not surprisingly, clear that Bleak would rather hang with his two ladies than be with me. We agreed that Bleak would show up at my hotel at seven the next morning, two-and-a-half hours before the deposition. I was highly skeptical that he would make it, but I had no choice in the matter.

At 6:45 I looked out onto the street area in front of my hotel and found Bleak and his driver asleep in their car. Bleak was wearing the same clothes from the day before. When I knocked on the car window Bleak came to, realized what he had to do, and accompanied me back to my room.

Bleak, who had never been deposed before, was a quick study and reviewed the facts of the case with me for an hour-and-a-half straight. We got to the lawyer's office for the deposition at 9:25. a.m. The questioning went on for over three hours. To my surprise, Bleak was one of the best deposition witnesses I had yet to encounter. He nailed his answers with authority and conviction.

Ultimately, the plaintiffs' case was dismissed for failing to adduce any credible evidence of access, and for the fact that the few similarities between the two songs, with respect to the common phraseology, "Around Here" and ""Round Here," were trite and found in numerous other songs. The lawyer for the plaintiffs learned a valuable if not costly lesson: copyright infringement cases in the music industry are difficult to prove or win.

58.
Credit Card Roulette

Las Vegas:

I represented Phil Gordon, the six foot nine professional poker player, television commentator, and author, for over three years when my travels finally took me to Las Vegas for the first time in 2006. Phil was gracious and offered to meet before dinner and gamble a bit before dining with some of his friends. Everyone in the Bellagio Hotel knew Phil and he was comfortable with his celebrity status. Phil said we should hit the blackjack tables and I agreed to follow. As Phil conversed with the attractive dealer on the other side of the table, he and I were treading water for a while, neither winning nor losing much. Then came a dealer change and so did our luck, mine for the better, Phil's for the worse. By the time we left the table, I was up fourteen hundred dollars and Phil was down twenty-six hundred dollars. Basking in my victory, I was tempted to but didn't offer to give Phil lessons in card play.

When we arrived at dinner, Mike Remlinger, a relief pitcher for the Atlanta Braves, and an event promoter named Bob were awaiting us. We downed some excellent Delmonico steaks, and Phil and Mike shared some high-end cabernet sauvignon to complement their meals. Mike entertained us with stories about life in the Braves dugout during major league baseball games and Phil told us of all the stars he had taught poker and blackjack, including Michael Jordan and Derek Jeter. Following our dessert and after dinner cordials, the check arrived. Phil announced it was time for credit card roulette. Since I was a novice, Phil had to explain what that meant to me. Each of the four of us were to throw our credit cards into the middle of the table. They would be shuffled, and the waiter would be asked to select one card. The owner of that card would pay the tab. Since I billed Phil five hundred dollars per hour for my legal services, I certainly could not complain about playing this game, but I still didn't want my number called. It was not Bob's lucky day and he got stuck with the tab.

Fast forward to New York two years later:

Jay Panda was at a point in time the youngest member of the Upper House of Parliament in India. I had known Jay since 1986, and although I acted as his family's attorney in the United States, our relationship was not professional. We were close friends. In the 1960s, Jay's father had created I.M.F.A. (India Metals and Ferro Alloys), a company that mined ferro alloys and now produced between three to five percent of the world's consumption of chrome. By 2007, I had been a guest of Jay's family in India on three occasions, had gone on tiger safaris and stayed with him on a remote island (Bitakonica), home to cobras, pythons, and monitor lizards. Given Jay's busy schedule between politics and his responsibilities with the family business, he frequently called me last minute for a get-together. This day would be no different.

It was a Wednesday morning, and Jay had just landed at Kennedy Airport with a governmental delegation from India. He called me at my law office and asked if I could rearrange my schedule to meet him and Sameer, another senator from India, for tea at five p.m. on Madison and 66th Street. Sameer was another wealthy young intellectual senator from India, representative of a new political movement taking place there. I met Jay and Sameer as planned, and we found a small patisserie to grab a snack and talk. After fifty minutes of energetic conversations about politics in India, cricket matches, tigers, and the economy, our waitress brought us the bill. Immediately Jay, Sameer, and I reached for our wallets and credit cards. Since Jay and his family paid for all my expenditures while I was in India, I had added incentive to pay the bill.

When it became clear that each of us was insistent in paying the bill, I decided to avoid an international calamity and explained to Jay and Sameer the principles of credit card roulette. Both Sameer and Jay thought it was a great idea and eagerly participated. The waitress came as I shuffled the credit cards. She selected Jay's and said she would be right back. Upon her return she had a quizzical look on her face and said that Jay's card had not worked. I shuffled the remaining two cards and she selected Sameer's credit card. Again she came back a few moments later and shook her head as it also had not been approved. Finally, I gave her my card, which she returned with the slip for my signature. I looked at Jay and Sameer and shook my head. "Here I was thinking I was hanging out with the cream of society from India and who knew I was really with two losers!"

Both Jay and Sameer laughed.

Jay looked at his watch and said they had to be off to the airport. I asked where they were going and why so little time in New York.

Jay responded, "We are off to Washington, DC, to see Condoleezza Rice to discuss India's nuclear initiative." I replied, "You had better make sure your credit cards are working."

59.
Eddie Palmieri v. Gloria Estefan—
The Rhythm Is Going to Get Ya

Eddie Palmieri, a five-time Grammy Award winner for Latin jazz, was and is an incredible piano player and raconteur. When I first met Eddie, he told me a great story. As a young performer, Eddie signed to a record label owned by the infamous Morris Levy, a true tough guy with an army of thug support. Eddie believed he was being under-paid on his record royalties. When he confronted "Mr. Levy" and asked for his money, Morris said to one of his soldiers, "pay the kid a few hundred bucks." When Eddie responded that he was due a lot more, and if he had to he would hire lawyers and accountants to get his fair share, Morris said, "There's a good place in the middle of the ocean for guys like that."

When Eddie came to me to represent him, it was concerning copyright infringement, rather than royalties. He had co-written and recorded a song called "Páginas de mujer" ("Pages of a Woman"), which had been released in 1981. The song contained a *coro* ("chorus") where the refrain "Oye Mi Canto" was sung back in response to var-ious chants, hitting a particular five-note musical progression in the process. In 1989, Gloria Estefan released an album entitled *Cuts Both Ways*, first in Europe, then in the United States, which contained a song entitled "Oye Mi Canto." While the body of the two songs, "Páginas de mujer" and "Oye Mi Canto" were dissimilar, the use of the "Oye Mi Canto" refrain accompanied by an identical five-note pro-gression existed in the *coro* of each song.

In May of 1991, Palmieri's complaint for copyright infringement was filed. In order to prove access, one of the two elements of a copyright infringement case, a plaintiff must show either (1) there is wide dissemination of plaintiff's work through record sales or radio airplay; or (2) by possession of a copy of the work by a third-party intermediary, who, by reason of his or her particular relationship with the defendant, would be likely to have shared or provided the work to the defendant. If an expert musicologist can credibly state that the two works at issue are "strikingly similar," access is presumed and need not be proven, because such a conclusion rules out a defense of "independent creation."

Access is often the most difficult component or element to prove in a copyright infringement case. Another pitfall in such cases when representing a plaintiff is that when you take a case on you have no knowledge of the universe of songs that were created prior to when your client created his work. When defending a case on behalf of a Top 40 artist/author you can easily spend over ten thousand dollars for an expert to do a survey of prior art to determine if any similarities between the two works are predicated upon pre-existing musical material. When initially confronted by a potential plaintiff, that survey and corresponding expenditure is not always undertaken or incurred.

Following the filing of our lawsuit, many radio stations played and compared the choruses of the two songs and, without the benefit of a prior art survey, opined on the similarity between the two songs.

During the course of the case, we learned that the words "Oye Mi Canto" had been used in songs that predated Eddie's song and that the five-note progression at issue had also been used in a few separate prior works, not combined with the words "Oye Mi Canto."

More than fifteen depositions were taken in the Palmieri case relating primarily to access and the creation of the two works, including Eddie's, Gloria's, her husband Emilio's, and his brother Jose's. On the eve of trial, US District Court Judge Robert Owen gutted our case by making a ruling that various important pieces of evidence for our case would not be admissible at trial. Accordingly, we lost the right to introduce evidence of radio airplay of Palmieri's song in the United States in general and Miami in particular, evidence that two close music industry associates/friends of Gloria's and Emilio's had copies of Palmieri's album, including the song, and testimony by Gloria's brother-in-law that Palmieri's song was played at Estefan family gatherings when Gloria was present. Based upon the judge's ruling we determined that we had insufficient evidence to go forward and the case was dismissed.

The moral of the story is that copyright infringement cases in the music industry are never as good as they seem to be at inception, and it is better to be an attorney for the defendants in most cases than for the plaintiffs.

60.
T.O.K. and the
Reggae Compassionate Act

T.O.K., a dancehall reggae group from Kingston, Jamaica, has released numerous popular songs and albums going back to the early 1990s. Depending upon who you ask, T.O.K. stands for "Touch of Klass," "Taking over Kingston," "Tribe of Kings" or "Theory of Knowledge." I did work for the band at various times during the 1990s.

In 1999, T.O.K. released the song "Chi Chi Man," which contained certain anti-homosexual lyrics and resulted in the band being targeted by various organizations promoting tolerance that were generally against violence in songs. Thereafter, a Western European promoter who was putting together a European Reggae festival and tour, in order to combat the public opinion fallout against various Jamaican bands who used lyrics that were less than ideal, asked all bands interested in participating with the tour to sign "The Reggae Compassionate Act," which stated:

The Reggae Compassionate Act
We, the artists of the Reggae community, hereby present this letter as a symbol of our dedication to the guiding principles of Reggae's enduring foundation ONE LOVE. Throughout time, Reggae has been recognized as a healing remedy and an agent of positive social change.

We will continue this proud and righteous tradition.

Reggae Artists and their music have fought against injustices, inequalities, poverty and violence even while enduring some of those same circumstances themselves. Over the years, reggae music has become popularized and enjoyed by an unprecedented audience all over the world. Artists of the Reggae Community respect and uphold the rights of all individuals to live without fear of hatred and violence due to their religion, sexual orientation, race, ethnicity or gender.

While we recognize that our artistic community comprises many different individuals who express themselves in different ways and hold a myriad of beliefs, *we* believe firmly that the way forward lies in tolerance. Everyone can keep his own conviction and we must receive respect for our freedom of speech as far as we respect the law, but it must be made clear there's no space in the music community for hatred and prejudice, including no place for racism, violence, sexism or homophobia.

We do not encourage nor minister to HATE but rather uphold a philosophy of LOVE, RESPECT and UNDERSTANDING towards all human beings as the cornerstone of reggae music. This Compassionate Act is hereby calling on a return to the following principles as the guiding vision for the future of a healthy Reggae music community:

Positive Vibrations
Consciousness raising
Social and Civic Engagement
Democracy and Freedom
Peace and Non-Violence
Mother Nature

Equal Rights and Justice

One Love

individual Rights

Humanity

Tolerance and Understanding

We, as artists, are committed to a holistic and healthy existence in the world, and to respect to the utmost the human and natural world. We pledge that our music will continue to contribute positively to the world dialogue on peace, respect and justice for all.

To this end, we agree to not make statements or perform songs that incite hatred or violence against anyone from any community.

ONE LOVE

_____

NAME IN PRINT _____ Signed: Artist

The irony was that no matter how harsh or anti-social the lyrics and sentiments expressed by the targeted reggae bands were, the promoter believed prior history could be washed away with the stroke of a pen.

T.O.K. was among many bands asked to sign the Reggae Compassionate Act. T.O.K. did not sign the Act but opted instead to sign their own drafted pledge called the "T.O.K. Compassion Act," in which they stated that: "We respect and uphold the rights of all individuals to live without fear of hatred and violence due to their religion, sexual orientation, race, ethnicity or gender."

T.O.K. is still making music today, entertaining audiences around the world.

61.
Jamaica:
Bob Marley and Shaggy

Bob Marley

Early on in Marley's career he signed a music publishing agreement with Cayman Music, a music publishing company owned by Danny Sims, where he assigned to Cayman a significant portion of his publishing revenue relating to songs he wrote. Following a number of Marley's successes with songs he had written, he mysteriously got writer's block and "no named" individuals in Jamaica began taking credit for songs he recorded and released. "No Woman, No Cry," "Them Belly Full," "Natty Dread," "War," and other hit songs were claimed to have been written by people other than Marley, mostly his friends and relatives.

Marley lived and surrounded himself with a violent group of people. Following a failed assassination attempt on Marley and his then manager Don Taylor on the eve of the Jamaican presidential election of 1976, Marley was airlifted out of Jamaica to Brazil. Over the next few weeks each person implicated in the assassination attempt was found mysteriously murdered in various parts of Jamaica. Nobody was prosecuted by the Jamaican government for either the assassination attempt or the reprisals.

Following the untimely death of Bob Marley in 1981, Danny Sims hired Parcher Arisohn & Hayes and brought a fraud claim against the Bob Marley Estate asserting that they had rights to many Marley hit songs written by him but credited to others. A central issue in the litigation was whether Sims knew or should have known years earlier he was being defrauded. If so, his claim would be barred by the Statute of Limitations. A claim for fraud in New York State must be brought within six years from its occurrence, or two years from when it should have reasonably been discovered, whichever is later in time.

During the trial, the lawyers for Cayman Music attempted to demonstrate to the jury the violent environment in which Marley lived in order to show that Marley's ghostwriting could not have been proven during his lifetime because Marley's cohorts would not have exposed any wrongdoing he may have done while he was still alive. Allan "Skill" Cole, one of Marley's managers, gave the following testimony at trial:

Q: Turning your attention back to 1980, at Miami, Florida, was there an incident there relating to Don Taylor?

A: Yes.

Q: Would you tell Justice Wilk and the jury what happened?

A: Well, it was three weeks before we started the US tour that ended prematurely [after Bob Marley became terminally ill]. And we invited Don to come over to Bob's mother's house for an argument, a little talk. Bob hadn't seen him in a couple of months. And he came, eventually he came after, took time for him to come. He was, he didn't really want to come at first when we spoke to him. But eventually he came. An argument developed inside of that room. and I closed the door. And it got rough. We got rough, and things like that.

Q: Got beaten up, right?

A: He got shaken up, beaten up . . .

Q: Did you point an Uzi submachine gun at Mr. Taylor?

A: It wasn't an Uzi . . .

Q: What was it?

A: It was an automatic .45, I think . . . There was a rifle around, but I didn't point no rifle.

Q: Now, I'm asking you specifically to tell Justice Wilk and this jury what, if anything, you did or caused to be done in the '70s to get Bob Marley's records played on the air.

A: Well, as I said, it was a difficult period in that time. And for us to get airplay, we had to put a lot of strength, what you call muscle, to get played from the various disc jockeys, and things like that. So it was my duty to see that these things happened. . . . Well, sometimes we had to go there and, you know, beat disc jockeys and deal with program directors and things like that. . . . So in that sense, we had to use a little muscle, some force, to get airplay. . . . Occasionally we had to beat—we had to beat disc jockeys. We had to send guys to—smash their cars or things like that. Threaten them. . . . If you didn't play our records you have to leave the station. You have to leave. Things like that.

Q: Did any person leave the station as a result of threats or beatings?

A: Yeah, quite a few people left the station during that year. Disc jockeys, I believe, program directors, left their jobs. Some went out to leave the country.

Q: And during that period of '76 were you then successful in getting Bob Marley's records played on radio?

A: During that period of time. . . . Yes. Well, that was the period of time that we got most of his number-one songs in Jamaica. In that period.

Q: And that was your job, both before Don Taylor and when Don Taylor came aboard, right?

A: Before and when he came.

The judge and jurors were on the edge of their seats during much of the testimony given by Mr. Cole and Don Taylor.

Despite the evidence of a violent environment in Jamaica during

Marley's life, the trial turned on an interview Mr. Sims gave to a book author writing on Marley's life, where in passing he acknowledged that he always knew he was getting "fucked" by Bob.

The jury determined that Mr. Sims should have brought his case sooner and the action against the Bob Marley Estate was dismissed. The case never determined the issue of whether Marley had in fact used ghost writers or not.

Shaggy—Really?

During the late 1990s through the early 2000s, I represented Paris D'Jon, a successful music industry manager and entrepreneur. Paris had been involved early on in the career of Jessica Simpson and had discovered the group 98 Degrees while in their infancy, after meeting them backstage at a Boyz II Men show in October 1995, when they were still an unsigned act. During Paris's term as manager, 98 Degrees rose to stardom. When they unceremoniously terminated his management agreement, I represented Paris and his management company, Top 40 Entertainment, in an arbitration against the band, which ultimately settled.

Shaggy, a.k.a., Orville Burrell, the Jamaican reggae fusion artist, scored it big with "It Wasn't Me," his breakthrough hit on his multi-platinum album, *Hot Shot* released in 2000 on MCA Records. Shaggy had been managed by Robert Livingston since the early 1990s. In part because Livingston had not been a supporter of "It Wasn't Me," Shaggy urged Livingston to bring in a comanager to assist in the management of his career. Enter Paris D'Jon. The comanagement relationship between Mr. Livingston and Mr. D'Jon, a difficult marriage, lasted less than a year. When Livingston ended his relationship with D'Jon, with no objection from Shaggy, D'Jon had to sue Livingston and Shaggy to get paid for his services.

When I got to depose Shaggy, who, as they say in the business, was a smart ass, Shaggy refused to acknowledge that Paris had acted as his comanager.

I asked him, "Why did you bring Mr. D'Jon with you when you went to meet the president of MCA?"

"I wanted him there to get me water when I was thirsty."

"Why did you bring Mr. D'Jon with you when you went to meet the president of your publishing company?"

"I wanted him there to get me water when I was thirsty."

"Why did you bring Mr. D'Jon with you when you went to meet your promoter?"

"I wanted him there to get me water when I was thirsty."

I interjected: "You're a pretty thirsty guy, aren't you? So does Mr. Livingston sitting to your left bring you water when you're thirsty?"

Shaggy looked at Mr. Livingston, smiled, and said, "Sometimes."

The deposition lasted three and a half hours.

Shaggy was evasive and less than forthright. It was clear that a jury would understand that as well.

The case settled a week later.

Being a smart aleck never pays off in the end.

62.
Twista—*The Guinness Book of World Records* Rapper

The year was 1999. Twista (Carl Terrell Williams) was one of the more well-recognized rappers of the day. In 1992, he was identified in *The Guinness Book of World Records* as the fastest rapper, being able to pronounce in rap 598 syllables in fifty-five seconds, a fact that would make any mother proud.

Twista had filed for bankruptcy protection and his former production company/record label, Creator's Way, a Chicago-based entity, sought to enjoin (stop) him from recording music for any other record label.

This was not the favorite case the bankruptcy court judge had on his docket, and to show his appreciation for all concerned, he ordered that the depositions of the two principals from Creator's Way, Lucky and the Legendary Traxster, take place on Christmas Eve, starting in the early afternoon until completed.

The only factual issues the court had to resolve were whether Twista's musical services "were unique and extraordinary" and whether Creator's Way had complied with its contractual obligations during the term of its recording agreement with Twista.

Before the depositions of Lucky and Traxster, I was apprised that they were tough guys and that Lucky's other nickname was "Pusher." Lucky and Traxster arrived at the offices of a midtown law firm around two p.m., having flown in from Chicago that morning. Each strode in wearing matching full-length white sable coats.

Traxster's deposition was uneventful. Then it was time for Lucky's.

Ten minutes into the deposition, after I had reviewed some of Lucky's pedigree, it was time to take him on.

Q. Do you go by any nicknames?
A. No.
Q. Do people call you any name other than your given name?
A. No.
Q. Sir, you are under, oath, do you understand that and you are subject to the penalty for perjury if you lie.
A. I understand.
Q. Sir, I ask you again, do you have a nickname?
A. No.
Q. Sir, isn't it true that you sometimes go by the name "Pusher?"
A. (Witness chuckles.) No.

A few minutes later, there was a break in the deposition and both Lucky and I were in the restroom at the same time. He turned to me and said, "That was a low blow."

When the deposition was over, Twista took me to the side and said, "You a bad motherfucka."

"Why?"

"That dude killed a guy in Chicago." I asked why he hadn't told me that before and he said he didn't think it was important. He then told me that I had misunderstood him. Lucky didn't go by the nickname "Pusher," he simply was a pusher. I left the deposition thankful to live another day.

63.
The Andy Warhol Estate

Andy Warhol, the American pop artist, was only fifty-eight years old when he died at New York Hospital in 1987 following a simple gall bladder operation. My firm, Parcher Arisohn & Hayes, was engaged by the Estate of Andy Warhol to pursue a wrongful death action against New York Hospital and others who treated him while he was there, and an action for the "pain and suffering" Warhol may have experienced before his death as alleged in our complaint. His claimed cause of death was overhydration due to the failure to monitor the intake and output of fluids, which were administered to Warhol both pre- and post-operative while he was in the care of New York Hospital and a private duty nurse.

In New York State, damages in a wrongful death action are determined and based upon the extent that "statutory distributees" (spouse, children, parents, siblings) depend upon the deceased for support. A spouse and children would generally be extremely reliant for support, while more attenuated relatives would not. If the victim had no earning capacity, the case would have no value. Ironically, if you went through a red light and accidentally killed a homeless man, the damages could be next to nothing for a wrongful death claim in New York. Whereas if you did exactly the same deed and accidentally killed Bill Gates, the damages could be billions of dollars.

Warhol had no wife, children, or remaining parents. If he had, given his life expectancy and prior history of creating hordes of collectible artwork, his death might have been the basis for one of the biggest wrongful death cases in US history. But he didn't. He did have two brothers, John and Paul Warhola, who remained in the Pittsburgh area after Andy moved East to the metropolis of New York.

Although Warhol apparently was in the custom and practice of gifting his brothers with pieces of his artwork, neither seemed very much impressed with it. In fact, one of Andy's nephews kept a number of canvasses of Andy's works, including a famous multiple Marilyn and Campbell's Soup Can, rolled up and stored under his bed for safe keeping.

When I first met John Warhola outside of Pittsburgh, I was struck by how different he was from Andy. Soft-spoken, conservative and not interested in the limelight, he was the antithesis of Andy. During our first conversation, he told me he didn't like coming to New York because "there were no good restaurants there." I asked what restaurant he liked and he replied, "Red Lobster." He was kind and uncomplicated.

Some of the top New York medical malpractice firms were against us in the case. Martin Clearwater & Bell, and Kopff, Nardelli & Dopf, were two of them. Every issue between our respective firms became a battle subject to a court ruling. When defense counsel demanded copies of Andy's personal diaries for the seven years leading up to his death, I was assigned the job of reading them and noting any instance when he discussed his physical condition or medical issues. The case was both interesting and complicated. There were medical, lifestyle, art world, productivity, and family dependency issues to name a few. I was given the opportunity to depose many of the doctors who treated Andy and defended representatives of the Estate and family members at their depositions as well.

The case plodded on for years and ultimately went to trial in the early 1990s after I had left Parcher Arisohn & Hayes for greener pastures. The newspapers clamored that the case had settled, but unfortunately I wasn't there when it reached the finish line.

64.
An Appellate Argument;
Facing Off Against Five Judges

The president of our client's company was a nasty bastard. He stepped on people as if they were expendable insects, playing head games throughout his power trips. He was missing the chromosome that facilitated editing your comments before you make them. In his latest foray into negativism, he allegedly told a number of company workers that one particular employee was a "faggot who probably had AIDS." If true, the claim would have been the president's one hundred and twenty-seventh indiscretion that year, but in any event led to a multi-million-dollar defamation lawsuit against him and his company.

The law of defamation covers injury to reputation resulting from false written (libel) or verbal (slander) communications to others. While opinions are not actionable, false statements of asserted fact that will expose an individual to hatred, contempt, shame, or disgrace usually are. False statements regarding someone's profession, sexual improprieties or inability, diseases, or criminal conduct that are injurious to the target of the statement form the basis for a defamation claim.

In a standard defamation lawsuit, the plaintiff must prove that a disseminated (published) statement to a third-party was false, was done negligently (without adequate investigation of the facts) or intentionally, and caused harm to the plaintiff. In the case of a public figure or celebrity, the burden of proof is higher, and the plaintiff must prove malice, which is an intent to do harm, or a reckless disregard for the truth.

Since truth is an absolute defense to a claim of defamation, truth is routinely asserted as an affirmative defense in any answer filed in response to a defamation lawsuit. Our case was no different. We denied the allegation that the company president ever said his employee was "a faggot who probably had AIDS," and then argued in the alternative that if such a statement was in fact made, it was truthful.

In order to prove our defense that the allegedly defamatory statement was true, my law firm requested that the plaintiff submit to a blood test to determine if he in fact did have AIDS. The plaintiff had admitted under oath having had sexual relations with another man. Opposing counsel moved to quash our application, arguing that our request for a blood test was an invasion of privacy and unjustified. The state court trial judge agreed, granting plaintiff's motion and setting us up for an appeal.

The Appellate Division First Department is located on 25th Street off Madison Avenue in an impressive Renaissance Revival limestone columned building built in 1896. An air of elegance and majesty exists before you even enter. Oral arguments take place in a large wood-paneled courtroom with a magnificent stained glass ceiling. Five judges sit on a raised seating area perched over their subjects. Lawyers who have oral arguments await their turn in an assigned seating area while visitors and others viewing the arguments sit in a separately designated gallery. Before the oral arguments of the day take place, the judges decide how much time will be allotted to the lawyers arguing each case. A "hot bench" is one where the judges pepper you with questions. A "cold" one allows you to go through your eight- to ten-minute presentation unscathed without questions. One never knows what to expect.

As the lawyer for the appellant, I was slated to present the initial argument on the appeal. I was twenty-nine and confident that my side had the better position. The plaintiff, who was seeking millions of dollars in compensatory damages, had put his physical condition in issue by claiming that the statement "he probably had AIDs" was false and we were entitled to find out whether such statement was true or not.

After an hour-and-a-half wait, our case was finally called, and I approached the podium to begin. Having barely finished my first sentence of introductory remarks, the feeding frenzy began. It was as if each of the judges had had double expressos and I had said something derogatory about their mothers. They assaulted me from the left, from the right, and straight on. My head pivoted to address each oncomer as they hurled their barbs at me.

To ward off the attack coming from five judges at the same time is no easy feat. My panel was so hostile to my position that one judge could not even finish lecturing or zinging me with a question before the next one jumped in.

"Counselor, this is one of the worst cases of bootstrapping that we have ever heard."

"How do you think you can justify this significant invasion of privacy?"

"Why on earth do you believe we should require the Appellee to submit to a blood test?"

"There are boundaries of decency that must be adhered to."

I swung back.

"With all due respect your honors, I beg to differ. If the alleged defamation was a claim that my client had called a woman a prostitute, I cannot see any reason why you would not have allowed me discovery to determine whether that woman had received money for having sex with men. Our case is no different. Here the Appellee put his physical condition in issue by claiming that the statement that he probably had AIDs was false. We should be entitled through the administration of a simple blood test to determine whether the Appellee has AIDs or not. Such a test is routinely administered when you seek to obtain a new life insurance policy."

One of the judges interrupted me. "Your clients put the Appellee's physical condition in issue when your clients' answer to the complaint asserted the affirmative defense of truth."

"May I be heard on that, your honor?"

"No! We have heard enough from you, counselor."

Sometimes rank-out contests end when one side declares himself to be the victor. Here, five judges did.

My adversary stood up and approached the podium. He asked if he needed to say anything. The panel said "No."

He sat down and our argument was over.

The decision on the appeal arrived five weeks later in a thin white envelope from the Appellate Division: "Affirmed," with no opinion.

We lost.

65.
The Zoppini Charm Bracelet—
A Settlement over Dinner

The hula hoop, the Pet Rock, and Cabbage Patch Kids, were all items that became fads due to their innovative concepts and great marketing plans. The same was true of the Zoppini charm bracelet. The brain child of three brothers in Florence, Italy, in 1995, the charm bracelets were created by customers who could choose charms made up of letters, numbers, popular designs, and icons to make a unique bracelet all their own. The cost of making the component parts of the jewelry was fairly low, and as long as there was sufficient demand for their goods, the Zoppini bracelets would be profitable.

The Zoppinis engaged Jonathan Ponsard to be their exclusive distributor and sales agent for the Zoppini bracelet line in the United States. Ponsard, through his ingenuity, helped transform the line from an unknown commodity in the United States into an extremely trendy fashion statement for the twelve- to twenty-eight-year-old demographic. Celebrity youths in the motion picture and music industry were given the bracelets for free and were photographed at posh events wearing them. Before long, their adoring public wanted to follow suit.

When Ponsard first purchased a Zoppini bracelet from the Zoppinis in 1998, they sold their wares only in Italy. From 1999 through 2001, Ponsard built a client list of 2,000 individuals and entities in the United States with sales over seven million dollars. By the end of 2002, gross US sales exceeded forty million dollars, but in 2003 they dropped to approximately twenty-nine million dollars.

By 2005, the relationship between the parties had broken down. The Zoppinis terminated their relationship with Ponsard and took over his client and distribution base, and a federal court lawsuit ensued. John Bradley, an attorney from Hollywood, Florida, who would ultimately become a great friend, brought me in to assist in his representation of Ponsard. The relationship between the parties was acrimonious at best. Everything was a struggle. If we said to the judge that it was sunny, opposing counsel said it was raining. After exchanging thousands and thousands of documents during pretrial discovery, it was now time for depositions. Our trial court judge had determined that two Zoppini brothers would be required to fly from Florence to New York to attend their depositions. At our final pretrial conference before the depositions, Judge Castel did a remarkable thing. He ordered the parties to have dinner together at the Smith & Wollensky steakhouse on the night before the depositions were to commence. John, opposing counsel, and I were all skeptical about this approach. Our respective clients literally hated each other and getting them in the same room seemed to be a recipe for disaster. That said, John and I understood that there was little downside to having the meeting and we would, at a minimum, get a good meal out of the encounter.

Mauro and Manuel Zoppini and their attorney arrived at Smith & Wollensky shortly after our arrival. John, Ponsard, and I had taken our strategic positions around the table. I played master of ceremonies and approached the Zoppini brothers and their attorney with hand extended to greet them and usher them to the table. They shook my hand half-heartedly but had no interest in shaking Ponsard's hand. When they sat down, there was a moment of silence, and it wasn't for the dearly departed. The temperature in the room suddenly turned frigid. We all silently stared into space. Despite the urge, I refrained from telling the Zoppini brothers that they had lived a "charmed life," I thought the pun would be lost on them.

I broke the ice by talking about how much I loved Italy and Florence in particular. I asked where their shop was and whether they had been to the United States before. I asked the brothers if they preferred red or white wine and quickly flagged down our waiter to order a few bottles of good Italian Barolo in their honor. Within twenty minutes everyone was drinking and talking. The room had warmed up a bit and I could now take off my coat. I suggested that the attorneys leave the table for a few minutes so our clients could talk. Despite some initial resistance from Ponsard and the Zoppini brothers, the lawyers were allowed to remove themselves and leave the battling clients to their own devices.

Settlements often are more feasible after the parties can vent in a cathartic way, getting their bottled-up frustrations off their chests. And this case was no different. The principals had a lot to say to each other. Watching from a distance, I knew that if no fists flew, we were safe.

Bradley, always the practical joker, called his partner in Hollywood and told him the meeting had gone terribly, a fight had broken out and that our client had been arrested. In actuality, after the third bottle of wine had been consumed, everything had gone swimmingly well. Progress was being made toward a global resolution of the dispute. After the consultation among the clients had been completed, Ponsard joined Bradley and me at a separate table so that we could talk in private to discuss deal points and the Zoppinis could do the same with their attorney. I was the shuttle diplomat between the parties. After almost four hours, a settlement was brokered and we all drank a final toast before our departure.

There is more than one way to skin a cat and apparently there are many ways to settle a case.

66.
Whose Meatloaf Is It Anyway?

In 1977, three smart gentlemen left the employ of CBS Records in New York to form the Cleveland Entertainment Company. Steve Popovich, the president of Cleveland Entertainment and a 51 percent shareholder in the entity was a visionary who had worked in the A&R (Artist & Repertoire) department at CBS. His co-owners were Stan Snyder, an outgoing and personable marketing and distribution man, and Sam Lederman, a savvy businessman. Cleveland Entertainment, doing business as Cleveland International Records, entered into a production agreement with CBS, in which CBS funded Cleveland Entertainment operations to locate, sign, and develop musical acts, committing to pay royalties on acts that earned money. Michael Lee Aday, professionally known as "Meat Loaf," was a twenty-nine-year-old performer with an incredible voice. As of 1976 he had had minimal success as a performer. He appeared on Broadway, in the movie *The Rocky Horror Picture Show*, and was a member of a regional band in California without any hits. Meat Loaf's musical style was unconventional to say the least, and numerous record labels turned down an album project entitled *Bat Out of Hell* that he and his songwriter friend Jim Steinman had worked on since 1972. In 1977, Steve, Stan, and Sam rolled the dice with Meat Loaf and signed him to their label imprint Cleveland International Records.

Bat Out of Hell was released in October 1977, and included the now iconic songs "Paradise by the Dashboard Light," "You Took the Words Right Out of My Mouth," and "Two Out of Three Ain't Bad." The album went on to sell more than 43 million copies worldwide.

In 1982, Steve, Stan, and Sam went their separate ways. Steve stayed in the record industry and Stan and Sam undertook different career paths. The three of them continued to receive royalties from CBS, then Sony Music Entertainment (CBS's successor-in-interest), and the three together exercised audit rights through their inactive business entity, Cleveland Entertainment, pursuant to the terms of their 1977 CBS production agreement. At no time were any of the assets of Cleveland Entertainment distributed to its three shareholders and, although it was no longer carrying on new business, it still had assets, including the right to receive ongoing record royalties from the sale of Meat Loaf recordings and its audit rights. Stan and Sam did not object to Steve using the name "Cleveland International Records" with respect to his own music business operations but they never formally assigned him any rights in the name, nor did they permit him to use the specific logo that had been used on the original Meat Loaf release for the *Bat Out of Hell* album.

In 2005, Steve individually won a 5.1 million-dollar jury verdict, plus interest, in federal court in Cleveland, Ohio, against Sony Music due to Sony's failure to place the Cleveland International Records logo on over ten million Meat Loaf CDs sold by Sony. With interest, but after deducting attorney's fees, Steve received in excess of four million dollars on his victory. Neither Stan nor Sam participated in that lawsuit, but as 49 percent shareholders in Cleveland Entertainment they requested their share of the recovery following a federal appellate court upholding the jury verdict. Steve rejected their overtures claiming among other things that: 1) Cleveland Entertainment was no longer a viable entity; 2) its assets had been distributed among the three share-holders; 3) he was the only one still in the music business and thus the only one damaged by Sony's conduct; 4) he alone had the rights to the use of the subject logo; and 5) Stan and Sam had waived any rights they might have had by not participating in the court case against Sony (even though they were never formally asked to participate).

I was retained by Stan and Sam in 2006 to sue Steve Popovich to recover the 49 percent in the Sony case which they were due. The case was vigorously defended by Steve and his lawyers every step of the way. We finally went to trial in December of 2009 in federal district court in Cleveland before Judge Nugent, a former US marine.

From the get-go, it was clear we were litigating in a hostile environment. Steve was a local hero in Cleveland, prevalent in the music scene, and affiliated with the Rock & Roll Hall of Fame. Our judge was on a first-name basis with him and would personally greet him each morning. Each day the courtroom gallery was filled with Steve's friends and relations. On one occasion, I asked the judge to take a short recess for a bathroom break and he said no, making me continue my questioning of a witness for another hour and twenty minutes standing behind the lectern with my legs crossed. Steve's entourage was laughing and hissing at me most of that time. Although our direct case with Sam and Stan as testifying plaintiffs seemed to go on decently, just about every court evidentiary ruling went against us and I was wondering why the judge wasn't calling my clients by their given names. The defense called a parade of witnesses who testified that Steve Popovich was in the world's eyes synonymous with "Cleveland Entertainment" and "Cleveland International Records," and that the subject logo was always more important to Steve than to Sam and Stan (which may have been true but was irrelevant).

During a trial, you have no way of knowing how various facts impact a jury's decision-making function. Evidence was adduced to show that at some point in time Sam and Stan learned of Steve's logo lawsuit against Sony and didn't think much of it. However, since they were never asked to waive or assign their rights in the claim to Steve, that too was irrelevant.

Two statements made by Mr. Popovich's attorney may have had some impact on the jury. The first was the term "black music" used to describe a genre of music in the industry in the '60s, '70s, and '80s. However, neither Mr. Popovich, as a witness, nor his attorney, gave any explanation as to what that term meant, and there were a number of African Americans on the eight-person jury. Also during Mr. Popovich's direct examination, his attorney asked him about a one-hundred-thousand-dollar bonus he received in 1978, and noted that was when "one hundred thousand dollars meant something." This statement was made to eight individuals who likely earned only between eighteen thousand dollars and forty-five thousand dollars annually per person depending upon their occupations.

My cross-examination of Popovich was rapid fire and heated. At one juncture he lost his cool and began screaming at me. Over time it became clear that Cleveland Entertainment did have assets, including the right to receive Meat Loaf-related royalties, audit rights, and the contractual right to require Sony to place the Cleveland International Records logo on Meat Loaf records or CDs. Popovich could not artic- ulate how or point to any document where this right was transferred to him alone.

When the jury finally got the case after four days of war, my clients were exhausted, shell-shocked, and not particularly hopeful of a verdict in their favor. The jury got the case late on Thursday. By Fri- day afternoon I had paced a rut into the marble floor of the court- house. At around four p.m. we were all called into the courtroom. The jury had reached a verdict.

There was silence in the courtroom as we awaited the judge's entrance. Stan and Sam were noticeably on edge. I could tell from my opposing counsel's swagger and overall demeanor that he thought he had won. Three lawyers were sitting at the defendant's table with Steve. The judge came in, sat on his bench, and told the bailiff to bring in the jury. Single file they walked in and went to their assigned seats, where they each had been sitting since Monday. The foreperson of the jury was asked if the jury had reached a verdict. He said yes and the judge directed the bailiff to bring him the three-page verdict form to read. If he read beyond the first page it was likely we won because damages were addressed on the second and third pages. After reading all three pages of the verdict forms, the judge gave the bailiff the form to give to the foreperson who was then asked to read the verdict. We had three claims: breach of contract, breach of fiduciary duty, and conversion of a corporate asset. One by one the jury foreperson said that we the jury find for the plaintiffs, and with that Sam and Stan were awarded 49 percent of the logo litigation recovery less Popovich's expenses in obtaining that result.

Stan and Sam were jubilant as they rose and hugged each other. Steve Popovich stomped out of the courtroom leaving his disillusioned and incredulous attorneys sitting stunned at the defense table. It was one of my better days in court.

There were two morals to this case. Never be overconfident when you try a case before a jury because you never know what a jury will do; and juries generally want to help anyone who appears to have been victimized or taken advantage of.

67.
Appearances Can Be Deceiving—
John Kerry with Jane Fonda

Within forty-eight hours, the photo of presidential candidate John Kerry standing next to Jane Fonda at a 1971 rally in Mineola, New York, protesting the Vietnam War had gone viral. The photo depicted Kerry, then a twenty-seven-year-old Vietnam veteran in army fatigues, back home from a tour of duty in Vietnam, standing in front of a podium ready to address a crowd on Long Island. To his left was Fonda, a well-known liberal and outspoken advocate against many governmental actions in the 1960s. The year was 2004, and the election between Kerry and George W. Bush was quickly approaching. The Kerry/Fonda photo had been posted by Richard Taylor, a resident of Michigan, on a conservative website known for social commentary, satire, parodies, and poking fun at Democratic liberal ideals and their candidates. Although removed after just forty-eight hours online, newspapers, magazines, television stations, and bloggers around the country republished the photo extensively. To moderates and conservatives, the Kerry/Fonda photo made Kerry appear more left-wing and liberal due to the association with Fonda and helped paint him as "anti-American."

Appearances can be deceiving. John Kerry and Jane Fonda never attended an anti-war protest together. Was the altered image social commentary, satire, parody, or fair use? The original photographer thought not.

Ken Light, the photographer who took the original John Kerry photograph on Long Island in 1971, who now lived in California, sued Richard Taylor in New York in 2007 for copyright infringement. He claimed that superimposing the image of Jane Fonda on his copy-righted image of John Kerry constituted a copyright infringement of his image which allegedly damaged him. Unfortunately, the merits of his claim were never reached as I succeeded in having his case dismissed on jurisdictional grounds since New York had no relationship to the claim.

68.
Sometimes Just Say No

The United States Copyright Act protects expression but not concepts, ideas or scenes de faire (sequences of events that result from the choice of a setting or situation). This legal principle is easier said than understood. An example will illustrate the doctrine. If you were to write a one-page summary or "treatment" for a potential show called *Seinfeld* and listed the character traits of the four featured characters as follows:

Jerry Seinfeld: a neurotic, self-doubting, stand-up comedian, who can't maintain a steady relationship;

Elaine: quirky, frequently puzzled, ditzy, critical, not easily impressed;

George: uncomfortable in his own skin and on occasion a buffoon, awkward, brazen, prone to say the wrong thing at the wrong time;

Kramer: a zany, slapstick goofy looking guy who always gets into trouble.

You would have *no rights* in the show called *Seinfeld*.

Your one-page treatment is simply a concept or idea that can be expressed differently a thousand times over. Nobody has a monopoly on concepts and ideas, and they are not copyrightable. But each *episode* of the show *Seinfeld* would be a different protectable and copyrightable expression based upon its plot line and dialogue.

William Roger Dean was a famous artist and designer who produced work in various media, including architecture, design, and painting. His work has hung in museums and he is well known for creating cover art and logo designs for rock bands, including the group Yes.

Many of his works were also featured in coffee-table art books.

When the blockbuster hit movie *Avatar* was released, many bloggers and commentators took to the Internet and opined that aspects of the film's ecosystem, including mountains, stone arches, trees, and wildlife, were similar to or copied from works done by Dean. To compound matters, James Cameron, the talented writer and film director whose works include *The Terminator* (1984), *True Lies* (1994), and *Titanic* (1997), was rumored to have been "inspired" by Dean.

Dean had created paintings with floating land masses, rock, moss, and trees ascending into heaven, solid arches in the mist, flat-topped trees, floating jungles, and flying dragons.

Cameron's movie also had floating land masses rock, moss and tree structures ascending into the sky called "Hallelujah, Mountains," stone arches, a "hometree" resembling a flat-top tree from Africa, a "tree of voices," and a horse-like creature called a "banshee" that could fly.

A side-by-side comparison of Dean's creations and Cameron's work revealed that no works were identical, but some had a similar "look and feel." However, one cannot get a monopoly on various ideas and concepts that can be expressed differently by a hundred different graphic artists. Floating land masses, stone steps covered in moss going into the sky, solid-mass arches, funny-shaped trees and animal con-figurations are general concepts and ideas.

After watching *Avatar* three times and doing a detailed analysis of Roger Dean's work, I politely declined the opportunity to represent Mr. Dean in a significant, high-visibility copyright infringement case against James Cameron and Twentieth Century Fox Film Corpora-tion, the writer/director, and motion picture company behind *Avatar*.

In September of 2014, United States District Court Judge Jesse Furman in the Southern District of New York dismissed Dean's copy-right infringement claim against Cameron and Twentieth Century Fox, that had been commenced by another attorney, finding that no substantial similarity existed between *Avatar* and copyrightable elements of Dean's artworks.

Judge Furman noted in his decision:

> Dean does not have a monopoly on the idea of floating or airborne land, an idea that has been around since at least 1726, when Jonathan Swift published his classic, *Gulliver's Travels*;
>
> The shapes of some of the land masses and features such as foliage on waterfall, to the extent these elements appear in nature, they are in the public domain and "free for the taking";
>
> Ideas such as flying dragon-like creatures, and other features taken from nature (stone arches, acacia trees, willow trees and colorful amphibians and reptiles) were not subject to copyright protection; and
>
> Dissimilarities between many aspects of the work outweighed any similarities.

When I read the fourteen-page court decision it reaffirmed my belief that sometimes the best decision you can make is to turn down taking a new case.

69.
Sometimes the Stars Align—
It's a Beautiful Morning

Eddie Brigati of the Rascals (formerly the Young Rascals) was a star in the 1960s. He coauthored "Good Lovin'," "Groovin'," "It's A Beautiful Morning," and "How Can I Be Sure." The Rascals, comprised of Felix Cavaliere, Dino Danelli, Gene Cornish, and Eddie, sold millions of records.

In 1996, Brigati did a copublishing deal with EMI Music Publishing, in which he permitted EMI to copublish and administer (control and commercialize) his copyright interest in various compositions for the twenty-eight-year renewal term of the copyrights (with respect to all songs written before 1978, there was an initial twenty-eight-year term of copyright followed by a renewal of equal duration, which has now been extended to seventy-five years in total). Marty Bandier, a significant figure in the business of music publishing, was the president of EMI at the time.

EMI commercially exploited and licensed the Brigati compositions for film and television for a period of time and then abruptly stopped making payments to Eddie. In connection with EMI's decision to turn off its stream of royalty payments, it claimed in writing that Brigati did not have the right to convey his copyright renewal rights to EMI because he did not own them. EMI strategically did not state who had such rights. It just so happened that based upon a tortured history of transactions involving the Rascals publishing catalogue, if Brigati had not owned the rights he said he did, a company owned by Mr. Bandier and Charles Koppelman would.

Based upon EMI's actions I was hired in 1999 to represent

Eddie's interest. Together with an incredibly savvy music publishing attorney named Harold Seider, who previously represented John Lennon during the time of the Beatles break-up, we drafted a complaint against EMI for breach of contract, and Bandier for tortiously interfering with EMI's contract with Brigati, based upon Bandier's ownership of another publishing company with Koppelman.

I was told in no uncertain terms by EMI's outside litigators that if I filed a complaint naming Mr. Bandier personally as a defendant, they would come after me for "Rule 11" federal court sanctions for frivolous conduct. In an effort to undercut the strength of our position, EMI rushed to the courthouse to strike the first blow, filing a complaint seeking a declaration that Brigati breached his agreement with EMI when he purported to assign it rights he did not have. Consistent with our prior resolve, we filed counterclaims against EMI and Mr. Bandier.

As the luck of the draw would have it, we were assigned to Federal District Court Judge John Sprizzo, a feisty, cantankerous judge who was quick to jump to conclusions and hard to move thereafter. Soon after filing our counterclaims, Judge Sprizzo ordered all attorneys to appear before him for a pretrial conference on a Tuesday morning.

EMI and Mr. Bandier were represented by Proskauer Rose, the powerful top 40, 700-man law firm. I was a partner at Goodkind, Labaton, Rudoff & Sucharow, a sixty-person firm. Proskauer Rose sent three lawyers to the conference. I went alone. We were the only lawyers in Judge Sprizzo's courtroom that day, unlike the Friday cattle call events that Judge Sprizzo hosted for numerous hours featuring a hundred lawyers waiting to be heard on forty different cases. Judge Sprizzo could often wake up on the wrong side of the bed and if he did you knew it quite fast. He had little patience for incompetence, game playing, or inarticulate attorneys.

As soon as Judge Sprizzo saw the three lawyers from the prestigious New York firm he commented that "things must be slow at Proskauer for you to have three lawyers here today." The EMI attorneys were asked to describe the case and their position first. One lawyer stood and gave an overview of the copublishing agreement between Brigati and EMI (making a few mistakes in the process), explained why Brigati had breached the agreement, and stated that it was an outrage and totally frivolous to have named Mr. Bandier as a party in this lawsuit. He went on to ask for permission to make a motion to dismiss the counterclaims we had filed against Mr. Bandier and the right to seek sanctions against my client and me for such outrageous conduct. When he was done, Judge Sprizzo said, "So, Mr. Caplan, what do you have to say for yourself?"

I started off by stating that in fifteen years of practice I had never named the president of a publishing or record company as a defendant in a lawsuit but that in this case my client had a good faith factual basis to believe that EMI's discontinuation of royalty payments to Eddie Brigati was based on a claim of entitlement to these royalties by its president Marty Bandier, in his capacity as a copyright proprietor in another music publishing entity. I went on to note that my adversaries had significantly misquoted and misapplied a key contract provision they had discussed before the court. Judge Sprizzo immediately cut me off and looked at my opposing counsel with concern. He directed that I take a seat and the Proskauer Rose spokesperson stand up and find the contract provision he had previously referred to. Sweat began forming on the lawyer's forehead as he began fumfering as he looked through the contract to find the provision he cited. To his chagrin, he came upon the clause at issue. "I'm sorry, Your Honor, I apparently misspoke. The clause is different than I had recalled." By this time the judge had located the page and paragraph and read it to himself. He was now in confrontation mode.

Judge Sprizzo peered done at the Proskauer lawyers and barked out his edicts:

"I will not trust another word from your side the rest of this case. There will be no motion to dismiss. There will be no motion for Rule 11 sanctions. Mr. Bandier's deposition will be the first one in the case.

"It appears to me that the plaintiff may have something to hide here. I want EMI to deposit 1.34 million dollars into court by next Monday. That is all. Have a good day, gentlemen."

I walked out of the courtroom in utter disbelief. Things like this don't happen. It was indeed a beautiful morning.

The case settled within the next seven days.

70.
An Ode to Ralph Mercado— "Music Industry Mogul"

The occupation listed on his death certificate in 2009 was "music mogul." These are the words I spoke at his funeral attended by the masses:

> Over the last twelve years I developed a deep affection for Ralph, who was a friend first and a client second. Confident and charismatic, Ralph touched the people with whom he interacted, including me. Ralph was proud, dignified, and secure in himself. He had a great sense of humor. Ralph's laugh was contagious and could fill a room with warmth. His smile could make you smile. Ralph could be charming, and he could be tough. He could be serious then playful. Throughout, Ralph had a lot of heart.
>
> The first thing that comes to my mind when I think of Ralph is family. They were the most important thing in his life. I remember my second meeting with Ralph, as his lawyer, before I really knew him. We were at RMM Records offices. He showed me picture after picture of his children and their families. As he described each photo he glowed with enthusiasm. Ralph was so proud of them and their accomplishments. Debbie, Demaris, Melissa, and Ralphie Jr.
>
> Ralph's love of Cynthia was deep and profound and her devotion to him unequaled. What Cynthia did for Ralph over the last two years is beyond description. To me, Ralph and his family were my family.
>
> Some people live a life but never truly live. Ralph could never

be accused of that. Ralph was an impact player, an innovator, a doer. Ralph had ideas and dreams and acted upon them. He achieved and nothing could hold him down. Ralph soared like an eagle. Ralph was a people person. He could relate to everyone, rich, poor, educated, uneducated. Ralph brought people together. He motivated people.

In 2002, Ralph took me to Cuba with him for a week. Each night we would go to the salsa dance clubs and the D.J.s would announce Ralph's arrival. Five hundred to eight hundred people would stand and applaud. On the third night I turned to Ralph and said, "What's all the commotion about you?" With a twinkle in his eye and his confident smile, he said, "Stick with me kid, you'll be alright."

Ralph, I am lucky to have stuck with you and by you. I am lucky to have known you.

God bless you. You will be missed.

71.
Thirty-Six Hours in Los Angeles

Every once in a while, as an entertainment attorney, things happen that make your head spin. On one particular short trip to L.A., I met with three clients and one potential client, all of whom I consulted with in the span of thirty-six hours.

First, I went to Santa Barbara to meet with Tom Steinbeck, John's son, and his wife Gail. Tom was a talented author and Gail was his adoring advocate. I was graciously welcomed into their home and we talked about art, literature, copyrights, and the Civil War. I asked Tom what it was like to be the son of John Steinbeck and he told stories of dignitaries and entertainers lining up outside his home in his youth to get an audience with his father. Tom talked of Albert Einstein paying a visit to his home when he was a young boy, bouncing him on his lap. Tom and Gail were interesting and charming. My five hours with them flew by, then it was time to head back to L.A., a two-and-a-half-hour drive.

I met Victor Willis, the original lead singer of the Village People, and his wife Karen, for lunch the next day. They each hugged me hello. At the time, I had been engaged by Victor to represent him in an audit dispute with his publishing company. I would later represent him, as I've recounted earlier in these pages, in a precedent-setting case to recover his copyright interests as a coauthor of twenty-four songs, many performed by the Village People, including the iconic "YMCA." Victor and Karen were both friendly and talkative. They had driven up from San Diego and were telling me details about their new home. Our time together was short but personable. We said goodbye knowing we would see each other in New York in the near future.

That afternoon, I went to the recording studio of Rodney Jerkins for a meeting. Rodney was and is one of the most talented music producers in the country, having produced for some of the top acts, including Michael Jackson, Whitney Houston, Mary J. Blige, Mariah Carey, Britney Spears, and Lady Gaga. His music and production work can be found on hundreds of millions of records sold and he has won four Grammys.

Rodney and I got down to business going over a number of issues in a case. When we were done, he asked if I wanted to hang out with him in the studio sound room for a bit. Rodney started tinkering on the keyboards while I sat, listened, and viewed his interactions with the sound engineer. In the course of twenty minutes, Rodney had created an incredible musical bed which would one day be the foundation for a hit song sung by a star. His music would be disseminated to Top 20 artists who would select the music they liked and sing over it, sometimes using Rodney to produce the track as well. I left Rodney's studio humming the beat to the song he had created only a few minutes earlier.

I met Big Chuck and one of his cronies three-and-a-half hours after our scheduled time to meet. Big Chuck gave me a bear hug lifting me off the ground, saying it's time to eat. "What's open in Beverly Hills at 11:30 p.m.?" I asked. "Anything you want," was the return volley. We went to Jerry's Deli, an all-night diner in Hollywood, to grab a bite. Two minutes after sitting down, the comedian Jon Lovitz walked in by himself and grabbed the booth behind ours. Jon ordered a peanut butter and jelly sandwich and a glass of milk. Big Chuck heard the order and roared with laughter, a bellylaugh approaching a volcanic eruption. "Did you hear that, just like mama used to make." Lovitz was unfazed and simply sat looking straight ahead. The waiter took our order a few minutes later and then returned, passing our table. He must have been a troublemaker because he made sure to show Big

Chuck that Lovitz's peanut butter and jelly sandwich on white bread was really just like mama used to make—the crust was cut off and the sandwich was cut into quarters. When Big Chuck asked Jon whether he was eight or ten years old, I turned pink with embarrassment. Poor guy didn't have a chance.

72

The Next Bar Stool Over—
The Hitman and the
Comedy Club Owner

We all make mistakes.

Peter "Fat Pete" Chiodo was a capo in the Lucchese crime family. He weighed between four hundred and five hundred pounds and killed people for a living. Fat Pete also liked to dabble in real estate investments.

RR, the owner of a comedy club in New York, was a purveyor of talent, an actor, producer, and entrepreneur. Rather than spend evenings sitting in his comedy club waiting to review the night's receipts, he would often hang out at a local bar a number of blocks away.

In the late 1980s, Chiodo and RR, strangers to each other, accidentally met in a bar not far from RR's club and began talking about real estate development. Before long they spoke of becoming business partners and jointly developing property in New Jersey. Chiodo's people would supply the capital. RR would use his business acumen to locate the property and devise plans for development. RR had no knowledge who Chiodo was. Ultimately a deal was consummated. Property was acquired in New Jersey and development began.

During 1990, Chiodo bungled a hit attempt on an owner of a concrete company and fell out of favor with the powers that be. In 1991, Chiodo was criminally charged with RICO racketeering violations and pled guilty in return for a lighter sentence, further displeasing his bosses who thought he might turn on them. On May 8, 1991, Chiodo, who was the target of a mob hit, was shot twelve times and lived, a benefit of his body weight. As a targeted man with no place to run or hide, he became a government informer.

RR learned of Chiodo's true identity when he received a call and learned that more than twenty-five FBI agents swooped down on the New Jersey real estate development and began digging in search of bodies.

Chiodo is said to have been the first sworn member of the Lucchese crime family to publicly break his vow of silence (omertá). In an unprecedented move, the "Family" ordered a hit on Chiodo's sister, who also survived the shooting, Chiodo would go on to testify against many leaders of the Genovese, Colombo, and Gambino families. Incredibly, some of the attorneys for the individuals prosecuted, subpoenaed RR to testify at the trial of their respective mob clients hoping that RR's testimony could undermine the credibility of Chiodo, a confessed mass killer.

It was my job as RR's lawyer to convince these mob lawyers that as an admitted killer, Chiodo's credibility could not possibly be further undermined or eroded by RR, who could only say that he was duped by Chiodo. As a result of my efforts, RR was not compelled to testify or appear in court and his life expectancy was extended.

73.
Frank Sinatra's Birthday Party with Ruth Ellington

It was mid-1995, I had been representing Ruth Ellington (Boatwright), the Duke's sister, in a dispute relating to her publishing company, Tempo Music. Mercer Ellington, Duke's son, and the Estate of Johnny Mercer were the other parties to the proceeding. The case involved the authorship of one of Duke Ellington's iconic songs, "Satin Doll," and music publishing royalties that Mercer Ellington claimed he was owed from Tempo. Ruth was a charming character, warm and engaging, who could tell stories about rubbing elbows with some of the most influential entertainers from the '40s, '50s, and '60s. Her husband McHenry Boatwright, an accomplished opera singer, was a thin, diminutive man who would often meet me at the door of their spacious Park Avenue apartment dressed in his pajamas, a terrycloth bathrobe, and house slippers. McHenry would hug me, speak in a whisper, and ask me how was life. Ruth was the whirling dervish of the two, on the phone, making social engagements, and chatting up a storm. She had the honored position of administering the copyright interest that her brother had in much of the music he created.

In early December, Ruth called me and asked if I had any interest in going with her to Frank Sinatra's birthday party at Tavern on the Green later that month. I didn't need to consult anyone for a second opinion and said I would be honored.

The valet parked my car. My name appeared on the guest list and I was ushered to my table. What a place to people watch.

I looked around the room and the tables were filled either with entertainers or Italian-American club members, a few of them "made men." There were men from the carting industry, concrete guys, builders, and restaurateurs. I recognized a few of them from their pictures in the newspaper. The rest of the room was comprised of television, motion picture, and music people. Tony Bennett was at the next table with a young girl who could have been his granddaughter but was in fact his date. Everybody was drinking and eating and carrying on, except Frank.

Frank was not well. Nancy was leading him around the room by his left arm while two behemoth bodyguards were hovering around him. He stopped by each table for a moment and exchanged pleasantries with his invited guests. Sinatra looked to be the shell of a man, barely aware of his surroundings. He had no life or sparkle in his eyes. Over time, many of his classic songs were playing in the background. "It Was a Very Good Year," "That's Life," "Mack the Knife," and "New York, New York."

The party lasted into the wee hours of the morning. Celebrities and dignitaries, including Frank, all stopped by our table to say hello to Ruth, who soaked up the attention. It was entertaining to simply be a fly on the wall.

74.
The Art of the Bluff

In poker, the art of the bluff is to have the same mannerisms when you have a good hand as when you have a bad one. Never let on by facial expression, body posture, or tone of voice any differences when you play and nobody will know when you are bluffing. Similarly, in life if you speak forcefully and with authority people will believe in you and have confidence in what you say or do. When you are knowledgeable about a subject matter no bluff is involved. On other occasions the bluff is intentional.

The year was 1991. I was on vacation in the Cayman Islands. The call from India came to the cruise ship I was on, and I was summoned to the ship's communication room to receive it. Dr. Panda, the chairman and chief operating officer of India Metals and Ferro Alloys (IMFA), greeted me with his usual friendly and endearing disposition. I had met Dr. Panda and his wife for the first time in 1987 when I was visiting their son Jay and was a guest at their home. Each morning Dr. Panda would come to breakfast in a beautiful silk robe carrying the *International Herald Tribune*. We would talk about global political, social, and economic issues. Dr. Panda had amazing insight into people, human nature, and world order. He treated me as if I was his third son. Spending time with Dr. Panda was both incredibly educational as well as spiritually uplifting.

Dr. Panda asked how I was, then quickly moved to the real reason for the call. He wanted to know if I could fly to New York and meet with him for an important meeting at Bear Stearns. IMFA owned the first privately owned electrical power plant in India and was interested in coventuring a new billion-dollar power plant in the state of Orissa, in India. Bear Stearns was targeted as a viable investment banker for the proposed transaction. While this type of transaction was not in my bailiwick, I had an excellent support team at the Goodkind, Labaton firm where I was on my way to becoming a partner. I was also a fairly quick study.

The offices of Bear Stearns could have been intimidating if you permitted them to be. Park Avenue, spacious, heavy wood furniture, billions of dollars of paper passing through their hallways. Bear Stearns was a major financial player in all markets including the so-called "emerging markets." Ace Greenberg, its chairman of the board, and Jimmy Cayne, its president, each had base salaries in excess of ten million dollars and were world-renowned players of bridge.

My associates at Goodkind, Labaton and I had a number of meetings at Bear Sterns to discuss and negotiate their engagement and now Dr. Panda wanted to close the deal. We were slated to meet with Jimmy Cayne, the Bear Sterns smooth-talking leader with much bravado and gumption.

Dr. Panda and I had briefly discussed our strategy before taking the short walk from my office to Bear Stearns. As soon as I told the receptionist that we were here to see Jimmy Cayne we were treated as if we were important dignitaries. We were escorted to a private waiting area outside Jimmy's office and a few minutes later we were led in to the Jimmy Cayne theatre.

Jimmy was sitting behind a huge desk. It made me think of Gordon Gecko in the movie *Wall Street*. Two of the company V. P.s were standing at attention, knowing who in the room they had to please. Jimmy was a natural storyteller. Robert Redford could have played him. After our introduction and some pleasantries, Jimmy went to work.

He told us about his recent trip to China where he and Ace played bridge with the number one and two men below the premier of China, with separate interpreters assigned to each of the four men for the purpose of the bidding process. He told us about the importance of emerging markets to Bear Stearns in general and to him in particular. China and India were places they wanted to "help develop" and make inroads.

Jimmy then moved to the subject of education. He looked at Dr. Panda and confirmed that he must have done well in school to build up his successful business. Jimmy then turned to me and said, "Brian, you must have done well in school, otherwise you wouldn't be here representing Dr. Panda." Since Jimmy was on a roll, who was I to correct him? I said, "Yeah, I did all right." He next looked at his two V. P.s noting that neither would be in the room with him if they hadn't done well in school. They stood in silence resembling well-adorned mannequins. Jimmy turned back to us. "You know, Dr. Panda and Brian, I didn't do very well in school." Before Jimmy could finish his sentence, I said, "Yeah, but you got an A in schmoozing."

Dr. Panda and the two V. P.s chuckled for a moment, but each quickly regained their contemplative composure.

Unfazed by my momentary interruption, Jimmy resumed his theatrics. Jimmy pointed to an eight-by-ten glossy photo framed on his wall and asked Dr. Panda if he knew who the three men were accompanying him. Dr. Panda, with his thick Indian accent said, "No, I do not know them." Jimmy plodded forward, "They are the members of my bridge club: Malcolm Forbes, Larry Tisch, and Ace Greenberg. You know the only difference between them and me?" Nobody replied. "The only difference between them and me is that they each own their own personal jets and I use the corporate jet."

Dr. Panda did his best impression of being politely amused at Jimmy's banter.

Jimmy was done entertaining. He was ready to get down to business.

The last proposal from Bear Stearns required IMFA to pay them three hundred thousand dollars in nonrefundable up-front money for their services and an 8.75 million-dollar success fee if they procured a strategic partner to fund the development of the new power plant in India in return for the receipt of a 49 percent interest in the project.

Jimmy reaffirmed that Bear Stearns would do what was necessary to effectuate a deal with IMFA and that he was confident that his team could both identify and procure for IMFA the joint venture partner they were looking for.

It was now my time to take the stage. With a serious poker face, I looked at Jimmy Cayne. "Dr. Panda and IMFA are honored that Bear Stearns wants to work with them. However, the up-front monies and success fees that Bear Stearns is seeking are unrealistic and unreasonable. Bear Stearns is not the only game in town and if we have to, we will go to Goldman Sachs right down the block. If Bear Stearns doesn't significantly reduce its demands for compensation, we will have no alternative but to go elsewhere."

Jimmy had temporarily lost control of the room. "So what are you proposing?"

Dr. Panda looked at me and gave a nod of approval.

"The bottom line is that IMFA is willing to pay you twenty-five thousand dollars up front as a nonrefundable fee and a 5.5 million-dollar success fee."

Jimmy hesitated then politely asked us to leave the room for a few minutes while he consulted with his minions. After about ten minutes we were called back into the room. Jimmy reached across the table and shook Dr. Panda's hand and said, "We have a deal. I will have my guys modify the paperwork and get it to Brian."

We thanked Jimmy for meeting and working with us on the finances of the engagement and then left the Bear Stearns establishment.

As soon as we were out of the building, Dr. Panda hugged me and said, "Brian, how did you do that?"

I said, "I don't know, but wasn't it fun?"

We both laughed and had a kick in our steps the rest of the day.

75.
The Cycle Sluts from Hell and the Groupie

I received the phone call at 1:45 a.m. Two members of the Cycle Sluts from Hell, an all-female rock band on the Sony label, had been arrested in a barroom brawl, and it was my job to go to their arraignment and get them out of jail. It can take in excess of twenty-four hours to process a new arrestee's fingerprints in Albany to determine if a suspect has a prior record or open arrest warrant for purposes of setting bail. However, an insistent attorney at the courthouse can often expedite the timing of an arraignment.

Living in northern Westchester at the time, I threw on a suit and while half asleep drove down to lower Manhattan, parked in an all-night open garage and made my way to 100 Centre Street, the criminal court building. It was three a.m., and only the scrambling night court attorneys and the lost souls, mostly relatives of incarcerated individuals, roamed the cold and colorless corridors of the courthouse.

With appropriate criminal court attorney identification I was given access to my two clients to assess their predicament and give them comfort that they would be released in the not too distant future. Being Sluts, they were proud of their early morning antics, but did want a good cup of coffee as soon as possible. Having completed my interview, confirming that they had no priors, I assured them that they would ultimately be released R.O.R. (released on one's own recognizance) without bail, but the timing would depend upon how fast their fingerprints were processed.

As I spoke to the Sluts, I learned that they were not the only ones arrested at a Greenwich Village watering hole. An overzealous groupie was also detained by the authorities. The Sluts asked me to represent their young fan as well. They only knew her first name, Josie. She was a "kid" being held in a large cell in the same multiperson holding facility. As the Sluts were being led back to their confinement area, I asked the correctional officer if I could interview "Josie," a young girl who was in the "holding pen."

Sitting in the interview area I waited five to ten minutes for my new client to arrive. Josie was eighteen or nineteen, tops, and looked like she hadn't slept for days. The rings under her eyes looked like a slice from a sycamore tree. There was alcohol on her breath, her hair was disheveled and her jeans torn. It became immediately clear that Josie was proud of her evening's accomplishment, arrested with the Cycle Sluts from Hell. What more could any eighteen-year-old blue-blooded American dream of? Clearly something to tell the future grandchildren. Josie, who lived with her parents, gave me her mom's name and phone number. It was then that I noticed what appeared to be an occasional twitch. When I asked if Josie was okay, she told me that she was fine, but had epilepsy and had missed her last scheduled dosage of anti-seizure medication. Josie said that in her exuberance to see the Cycle Sluts perform she forgot her meds at home. The price of poker just went up. I told Josie that I would immediately call her mother and everything would be okay.

Pacing back and forth I waited for the courthouse pay phone to be free. It was now 5:30 a.m. Josie's mom answered the phone and I politely identified myself, explained the situation to her and did my best to calm her anxieties. She lived in Southern New Jersey and said it would take her at least an hour and forty-five minutes to get to the courthouse with Josie's medications. I was informed that the longer Josie went without the meds the more violent and dangerous her seizures would become.

I popped my head into the arraignments office to check on Josie and the Sluts' paperwork and found, not surprisingly, that nothing had come in yet.

Josie's mom arrived shortly after 7:15 a.m. and I immediately took the epilepsy medication to the corrections officer I had been interacting with earlier. It was then that I learned a lesson in criminal court protocol. If you are arrested and do not possess health-related medication on your person, the Department of Corrections personnel can't pass it along from friend or family as they have no way of knowing what substance they are providing to a detainee.

Trying to maintain a calm, cool, and collected demeanor, I reconnected with Josie's mom and told her I would make an application to the sitting judge on the bench in the one criminal court part that was open at 7:40 a.m. I went to the assistant district attorney and separately to the courtroom clerk and described the situation that I wanted to bring to the judge's attention. They understood the immediacy of the situation and facilitated an audience with the judge while other matters were put on hold.

To my chagrin the judge told me that under no circumstances could medication, not found on an arrestee's person at the time of arrest, be given to court personnel to be passed on. A criminal court defendant either would have to wait till they were arraigned and released, or they could request an in-custody transfer to a hospital emergency room, in this case Downtown Beekman Hospital, for purposes of a health assessment and the prescription of needed medication. The latter approach was voluntary and had to be requested in writing by the incarcerated individual.

It was now between 8:30 a.m. and nine a.m. and I went to see Josie again. She looked worse than before and confirmed that her seizures were happening more frequently now. I told her that her mother was here, she had her meds, but we couldn't get them to her. I further informed her that she likely wouldn't be arraigned for hours. As we were talking, Josie's body began to contort, her eyes blinked, and her head tilted at a sharp angle. I was at a loss for words. I told Josie that she needed to sign a form that I would procure for her and go to the hospital to get the meds she needed. Without even thinking about the alternatives, she told me no way was she leaving the company of the Cycle Sluts. I implored her to change her mind, but she was stubborn as a mule.

Next, I met with the Sluts and asked them to convince Josie to go to the hospital. Their urging fell upon deaf ears.

With Josie's mom in tow, I went back to the judge and, as if my own life depended upon it, asked her to issue an order compelling and directing that Josie be sent immediately to the hospital for evaluation and medications. The judge refused to do so, saying that Josie had to request it. Not one to accept "no" as an answer and getting frustrated with our judicial system, I remarked to the judge that if she waited till my client's seizures became so violent that she passed out and struck her head in an unconscious state my application could be moot. The judge, not too pleased with me, admonished me for being too argumentative. After my scolding, she noted: "Counselor, I understand your predicament, but my hands are tied."

Meanwhile, the epileptic seizures were beginning to mount in both frequency and intensity. I checked in with Josie again and, even though she was fighting through the seizures, she was steadfast and insistent that a bulldozer couldn't separate her from the Sluts.

It was now 12:15. I don't know if I had ever felt more powerless as an attorney. I had a frantic mother and an obstinate child on my hand. I had kept the Sony Music representative informed of what was going on since ten a.m., but there was nothing they could do either.

From 12:30 p.m. to 3:15 p.m. I went into the arraignments office every twenty minutes to check on the status of my clients' paperwork.

My pacing was wearing a rut into the marble floors of the courthouse. I aged. So did Josie's mom.

At 3:35 p.m., twelve hours since I first arrived, the paperwork finally came, and we were assigned to a different judge for our arraignment. I ran to the courtroom with Josie's mom trailing behind me. I filed my notice of appearance, handed it to the court clerk, and asked him to call my cases as soon as possible. In the meantime, I introduced myself to the A.D.A. and told him who I represented and why time was of the essence. Before you knew it, my clients were called before the judge and, after a short presentation made by me and with the acquiescence of the A.D.A., they were all released with no bail. The Sluts hugged me and Josie hugged her not-too-happy mom. With a sip of soda, Josie washed down her anti-seizure meds and I breathed a huge sigh of relief.

76.
The Band Did Not Play On

Pink Floyd.
Simon & Garfunkel.
The Beatles.
The Eagles.
The Young Rascals.
Crosby, Stills, Nash & Young.

What do each of these bands have in common?

They all were successful and they all eventually broke up.

The relationship of band members to each other is a fragile one, akin to a marriage. When it doesn't work out after a long honeymoon period, sparks often fly. Inflated egos, jealousy, and conflicting views of each member's importance to the band combine to create an environment of animus in the context of the divorce of band members.

Unfortunately, new bands do not enter into prenuptial agreements and the average start-up band does not even have the financial wherewithal or motivation to have a written partnership agreement drafted or adopted, which would otherwise delineate the rights of leaving members. An average band has a number of income streams: record royalties, publishing revenue (depending upon who writes the compositions that the band records), touring income, and merchandising income. In addition, unless otherwise contracted away to another party, the band has an interest in the band's name/trademark and any related logos.

Without a written partnership agreement, a band's relationship is terminable at will, which means that any band member can discontinue the relationship and an aggrieved band member will only have a right to an accounting and his or her share of partnership assets. Valuing a band's name/trademark and logos is not an easy task and may lead to further friction. If split agreements delineating each partner's copyright interest in band compositions were never executed, songwriter contributions can also be at issue.

Under most state laws, partners and shareholders in corporate entities normally owe fiduciary obligations to each other such that one band member cannot take actions in his self-interest to the detriment of another band member. If a band member is kicked out of a band shortly before a big payday from a record label, tour promoter, or merchandising company, he may well have a claim of breach of fiduciary duty against the rest of the band. Over the years, I have represented at least twenty bands or former band members in these sorts of disputes.

Case Scenario 1

A musician was affiliated with a band for a few months, years before they had achieved any success. Following the release of the band's album that went platinum, the musician claimed to be a coauthor on a number of the band's released compositions and to be a co-owner of certain master recordings recorded by the band because he claimed he either performed on these recordings or the recordings were a "partnership asset."

Some bands agree that any composition written by a band member and performed by the band will be a band partnership asset split equally among the band members. One for all, all for one. Ultimately, this approach will backfire unless all band members participate equally in the creation of all compositions recorded by the band. Otherwise the predominant songwriter will feel he is getting the short end of the stick. A more pragmatic approach is for each contributor to receive his pro-rata share of the underlying composition based upon what he or she has actually created. The problem arises when there is no split agreement and the band breaks up or ejects a member within three years (the statute of limitations for joint-authorship claims) of the creation and commercial release of a song. In order to qualify as a coauthor, one must contribute copyrightable subject matter to the ultimate finished work and intend that such contribution will merge into the completed work. Once a composition's melody and lyrics are written, experts can differ as to what additional contributions are subject to copyright protection.

In our case, the musician did not contribute any copyrightable subject matter to the songs he performed during rehearsals in the developmental stages of these songs. He had no role in the creation of the melody or the lyrics to these songs and his musical accompaniment generally followed the melody already created. His coauthorship claim therefore had no merit. Any copyright ownership claim he presented based upon his alleged status as a partner in the band would also fail as the Copyright Act requires any transfer of a copyright interest to be in writing to be enforceable. During the musician's short affiliation with the band, no written document was signed by the band members to confirm that any copyright interest in the compositions created by other band members were being transferred to the musician.

When a band member is kicked out of a band the partnership relationship among the band members, if any, ends. Accordingly, bands that have record deals with record companies, and who have been working in the studio on their next record release, often recut their recorded tracks to take out the departed member's performances. This eliminates his entitlement to a record royalty participation on the band's upcoming release.

Since the musician's performance was not included on the actual sound recordings released because his contributions had been re-

recorded by another musician, he was not entitled to any royalty participation on the sale of the band's album and singles. The musician's partnership claim to a piece of these revenue streams also failed, because even if he were to prove that a short partnership existed, which was dubious at best, the final master recordings were created after the alleged partnership relationship ended.

Case Scenario 2

The heavy metal band had been in existence for decades. Its founding members numbered five and its touring members numbered an additional eight. The band's logo, recording agreement, merchandising deal, publishing interest, and touring company were all band assets. The eight road warriors for the touring schedule were paid as independent contractors and did not participate in the band's other income streams.

Over time friction developed between one of the five founding members and the other four. To his chagrin, he was unceremoniously ejected from the band under the pretext that drug/alcohol use was interfering with his band responsibilities. Conveniently the ejectment took place shortly before large advances were due from the band's record company, merchandising partner, and tour promoter.

The former band member now had claims to his share of partnership assets, including the band's name and associated logos, and a claim for breach of fiduciary duty against the other four founding members who were arguably trying to cut him out of a piece of the record, touring, and merchandising revenue advances to be earned within six months of his ejectment. Accountants were engaged to assess the value of the claims and the attorneys negotiated a settlement to avoid a very expensive public divorce if a lawsuit was to have ensued.

77.
The Young Rapper's Fork in the Road

TJ, the young rapper from the projects of Staten Island, had made a name for himself with his first record release. He drove around in an eighty thousand dollar automobile, wore fancy jewelry, and everybody knew his name. Left behind, but not far behind, were the projects, the tough life—drugs, guns, violence, one-parent households—with too many children to feed, food stamps, frustration, high-school dropouts, and a one-way ticket to nowhere. Dead ends were around every corner.

TJ was different. He had a sparkle in his eye and a bounce in his step. An inner charm and magnetism set him apart. He knew he would get out and did. He would not follow in his father's footsteps, a father he did not know.

I got the call to represent TJ on a Thursday and was told that his next court appearance was ten days down the road. Disorderly conduct and resisting arrest were the charges. Driving around in a fancy car worth more than a rookie officer's annual salary, he was a target for our establishment's finest, the New York City Police Department. On the fourth occasion, he was pulled over and asked to step out of his car and frisked without probable cause. He mouthed off to his two white assailants. The only problem was they were dressed in blue, carried guns and had badges. Invoking his first amendment right to complain caused him to temporarily lose his right to remain free.

By virtue of his clean criminal record and my persuasive ability, I was able to convince the assistant district attorney, with a little help from our assigned judge, to drop the trumped up charges against TJ.

On our drive back to my office, TJ confided in me how frustrated he was with the system. He suggested that he was considering buying a gun since many of his friends had them and the cops were busting his chops whether he had a gun or not. I emphatically told TJ that buying a gun would be a huge mistake, to look at his accomplishments to date and to not possibly throw it all away in response to a number of shakedowns by bad cops. I confided in TJ about some of my own youthful experiences to help gain his trust. I told him that the white cops would love for him to buy a gun because they would then have a valid basis to arrest him after they pull him over. When I was done with my lecture, TJ reluctantly agreed that he might be better off not buying a gun.

Four months later, the front page of the *New York Post* had a photo of a hip-hop mogul who had been arrested for gun possession. Later the next day my phone rang. I picked it up. It was TJ. He wanted to thank me for the stern advice that I had given him.

Epilogue:
Life Lessons I've Learned That Guide Me

All relationships need to be nurtured like children and plants.

Show me a guy that doesn't mind losing and I will show you a loser.

Supply and demand starts from breastfeeding onward.

Nobody can take your integrity from you, but you can easily give it away.

If you think that you are the smartest person in the room, you still have a lot to learn.

We are constantly shaped by our experiences and can change and evolve no matter how old we are.

Laughing makes you live longer.

Don't take yourself too seriously.

When a rapper says, "We got beef," it is not because he is a spokesperson for the American Cattleman's Association.

Don't ever let anybody piss on you and then call it water.

If you can get along with billionaires and beggars, you can get along with anyone.

Positive thinking is easier on the body and mind then is pessimism.

When I am asked if the glass is half empty or half full, I see it as three quarters full.

Generosity of spirit is contagious.

Don't ever feel sorry for yourself; it's a waste of time.

As a lawyer, if you build personal relationships with people, the business will follow.

Don't blame your actions as an adult on your life as a child.

If you provide positive reinforcement to others, it will come back to you.

Cross-examining a witness at a jury trial is a lot like Viagra; if it lasts more than four hours, call a doctor.

There are a handful of abilities that make a good litigator:
• Intelligence and the ability to be analytical and articulate;
• Being confident, charismatic, and personable;
• Being empathetic;
• Having the ability to assess what makes your client tick and talking their language, as we all hear differently; and

• Controlling your client's ego and expectations, never letting yourself get pushed around.

I am fortunate to have learned and continue to learn life lessons that help guide my actions.

As a juvenile delinquent, I made many mistakes based upon poor judgment and impulsive, self-centered behavior. As a doctor of jurisprudence, zealously and effectively representing clients, while maintaining ethical integrity, has been my driving force.

Lightning Source UK Ltd.
Milton Keynes UK
UKHW020643260722
406393UK00009B/1052

9 780578 626970